HIDDEN ARGUMENTS

Hidden Arguments

Political Ideology and
Disease Prevention Policy

Sylvia Noble Tesh

Rutgers University Press
New Brunswick, New Jersey

For my daughters
Diana and Carolyn

Fourth paperback printing, 1996

Earlier versions of chapters one, four, and five appeared in *The International Journal of Health Services* (1982, 1986, and 1984); reprinted courtesy of Baywood Press. An earlier version of chapter two appeared in *the Journal of Health Politics, Policy and Law* 6 (1981); reprinted courtesy of Duke University Medical Center.

Library of Congress Cataloging-in-Publication Data

Tesh, Sylvia, 1937–
  Hidden arguments.

  Includes index.
  1. Medicine, Preventive—Government policy—
Political aspects.   2. Science—Political aspects.
3. Diseases—Causes and theories of causation.
I. Title.
RA394.T44   1988   362.1'0425   87-9866
ISBN 0-8135-1269-7

British Cataloging-in-Publication
information available

Contents

Acknowledgments

It was my professors at the University of Hawaii who first introduced me to postmodern philosophy and thus to the theoretical propositions with which I began writing this book. I am grateful to all of them for the intellectual climate they provided, for their insistence that theory and facts could not be separated, and for their enduring friendship, especially Ben Kerkvliet, Adrian Kuzminski, Deane Neubauer, and Mike Shapiro.

Most of this book was actually written at Yale, while I was at the Institution for Social and Policy Studies' Center for Health Studies. I am extremely grateful to Ted Marmor, who then directed the center. He continually encouraged and supported my work, was happy to discuss my developing ideas, and created the kind of environment where colleagues become friends. In addition, both Ed Lindblom and Dick Nelson, who headed ISPS during my years, read portions of the manuscript in various stages of preparation (indeed, Dick read virtually all) and gave me excellent advice about revisions. Especially important, Terry Eicher made sure that I had all the technical assistance anyone could want and constantly cheered me on. I wish to thank all of these people. Their help was particularly generous because their ideas on health politics sometimes differ markedly from mine. I also owe thanks to the Henry J. Kaiser Family Foundation for their grant to the Center for Health Studies, which supported much of the research for the book; to the National Institute of Mental Health for the fellowship they awarded me to work on stress; and to Phil Leaf for his generous help as project director for the NIMH grant.

Earlier versions of several chapters appeared first in professional journals. The basic form of chapter one, and most of chapters four and five, were originally published in *The International Journal of Health Services* 12(1982), 16(1986), and 14(1984). Chapter two is an updated version of an article I wrote for *The Journal of Health Politics, Policy and Law* 6(1981). My thanks go to the publishers of those journals.

In addition, a special acknowledgment is due to Virginia de Rojas in Havana, and to her colleagues at the Instituto de Medicina Tropical, who invited me to Cuba, cheerfully steered me around, and patiently answered my constant questions.

I also want to thank all the members of a two-year-long ISPS seminar on interpretive methodology, as well as Rob Crawford, Leslie Rado, Jody Sindelar, and Evan Stark for sharing with me their ideas and listening to mine.

It is particularly gratifying to be able to acknowledge the help of my daughter and my mother. Carolyn Tesh spent many hours carefully reorganizing the citations and Pat Noble lovingly proofread the entire book.

Finally, many thanks go to my husband, Bob. He called my attention to health and disease in the first place, took a keen interest in this project from the beginning, supplied several hundred reprints of the scientific literature, and has participated with me in many hidden arguments.

HIDDEN ARGUMENTS

Introduction

This book is about the influence of political beliefs and values on disease prevention policy. My thesis is that behind debates about such questions as the toxicity of environmental pollutants, the hazards of smoking, and the health effects of cholesterol lie other, hidden arguments. These arguments are more fundamental: What is the legitimate source of knowledge? What is the nature of human beings? And what is the ideal structure of society? Firmly but often unconsciously held answers to these questions guide scientists, policy makers, and ordinary citizens alike to different constellations of facts about the causes of disease and, hence, to different preferences for prevention policy.

It is not my purpose, however, to lament the unfortunate influence of values and beliefs on policy making. Nor is it to deplore the presence of extrascientific assumptions in research on disease causality. The point is not that values contaminate policy, not even that values contaminate science. Instead there is an inextricable interrelationship between facts and values, both in the search for the causes of disease and in the process of developing the best preventive policy. I argue not that values be excised from science and from policy but that their inevitable presence be revealed and their worth be publicly discussed.

Because disease prevention policies are always based on assumptions about disease causality, this book concentrates on questions of causality. It examines three principal topics: (1) the influence of politics and economics on causal theories, (2) the effect of dualism on causal theories, and (3) the consequences for policy making when facts and values are not kept conceptually distinct.

Chapters one through three address the first of these topics. Chapter one shows that during the nineteenth century, four theories to explain what we now call infectious disease vied for predominance. They all acquired meanings beyond the narrow question of illness, each becoming linked to a different position about the desirability and direction of social change. Thus it became impossible to advocate one theory of causality over another without simultaneously implying a position in a larger political debate. Chapter two turns to the twentieth century. Today three explanations for chronic disease, remarkably similar to the nineteenth-century accounts, also compete for acceptance. Each explanation implicitly assigns responsibility for prevention to a different group of people, thereby taking a position in the ongoing political debate over which features of contemporary society are immutable and fixed, which are transient and amenable to redress. In chapter three I reexamine these causal theories from a more critical perspective. I point out that during both the nineteenth and twentieth centuries reconciliatory-minded people have proposed a multicausal explanation for disease, attempting to circumvent the arguments each single theory produces. I then argue that multicausal theories turn out to be worse than monocausal theories. They are ineffective guides for policy and lend themselves to dishonest representations of reality. At the end of chapter three, I describe what I call a structural view of disease causality. Such a perspective, first proposed in the middle of the nineteenth century, might provide a better basis for prevention policies, even though this more radical position has several theoretical and practical drawbacks.

In the next three chapters, I move from the influence of politics on theories of causality to my second topic, the influence of dualism. These chapters are case studies of dualistic assumptions distorting analyses of causality. Chapter four concerns the distinction between the individual and the society. It takes up the proposition from the earlier chapters that disease prevention policies that place responsibility on individual men and women are unjust. The case in point is Cuba, where a vigorous health promotion campaign does precisely this. The chapter proposes that progressive policy analysts who favor shifting responsibility for disease prevention from the individual to the society misunderstand the dialectical relationship between people and their social world. In that relationship each element creates the other, and a disease prevention policy that ignores this reality risks depriving men and women of an opportunity to participate as full citizens in their society.

The second case concerns the distinction between objectivity and subjectivity. Whereas chapter four discusses the principles supporting the objections to a particular sort of prevention policy, chapter five discusses the beliefs supporting a particular kind of research. It centers on the 1981 claim by air traffic controllers that their job caused disease because it was stressful. Showing that scientific studies of stress necessarily distort the reality they investigate by attempting to separate objective from subjective phenomena, the chapter describes how those investigations invalidated the controllers' claim that their job conditions were stressful.

The third case concerns the distinction between science and politics. Similar to chapter five in that it examines scientific research, chapter six concentrates on the argument about Agent Orange. It first describes the political meanings that Agent Orange has acquired; then suggests that the best way to understand why scientists disagree about the toxicity of this herbicide is to explore the political values they bring to the study. This chapter reviews and discards the usual explanations for scientific disagreements, showing instead that science, because it does not exist without scientists, necessarily requires value-filled human decisions at every step.

In the concluding chapter of this book, I consider my third topic, the consequences for disease prevention policy-making if values and beliefs are inextricably interrelated with scientific studies of the causes of disease. I suggest that the inherent presence of subjective judgments in science and in policy does not rob these two endeavors of entitlements to rationality or of standards of excellence. For if facts and values are interrelated, then neither can claim for itself complete objectivity or complete subjectivity. Each has elements of both. There are, therefore, objective reasons to favor, in given situations, certain beliefs and values over others, for these subjective judgments have objective content. In the case of disease prevention, I argue, some beliefs about the legitimate source of knowledge, the nature of human beings, and the structure of the ideal society may be better than others because they engender less disease.

CHAPTER 1

Nineteenth-Century Debates

In industrialized countries today a number of academics, public health officials, and citizen activists tell us we need a new public health revolution. They analyze accumulating data on the health effects of air and water pollution, occupational toxins, food additives, and radiation and conclude that only an environmental approach to disease prevention will control our major diseases. Labeling the usual germ theory–based public health measures narrow and limited, they remind us of the nineteenth-century sanitary reforms. A hundred years ago, they point out, a few reformers who thought of the environment as the cause of disease instituted a remarkable array of measures intended to make that environment healthier. At the height of laissez-faire capitalism, Europeans and North Americans passed laws to provide clean water and clean air, adequate disposal of both factory and domestic wastes, healthier working conditions, and, later, safer food. These reforms were aimed at eliminating what we now call infectious disease. Today, the new environmentalists argue, we need a similar approach to the control of the chronic diseases—cardiovascular disorders and cancer— that have steadily increased with industrialization and now account for almost two-thirds of deaths in Europe, the United States, and other developed countries.

The barriers to controlling chronic diseases through environmental changes seem enormous. Scientists debate endlessly over

7

what, exactly, is toxic to our health; government agencies charged with regulating dangerous industries suffer from nearly fatal institutional weaknesses; and the public, bombarded with reports on environmental health hazards, resorts to paralyzing fatalism. It is instructive to look again at the nineteenth-century sanitary reforms and ask how they came about.

The standard answers given in most medical and public health textbooks rest on the germ theory of disease causality. On the long journey from ignorance to enlightenment and just before the role of microorganisms was clearly understood, mankind made a short detour to an environmental (or miasma) theory of disease. The theory turned out, of course, to have been wrong, for it held that disease is caused by the odor of decaying organic material. But fortunately the public health policies it engendered were fairly effective in controlling epidemics, and eventually scientists discovered the real, microscopic cause of disease.

This characterization of knowledge as a linear process probably owes much of its popularity to the comfort it provides. But there is little evidence that the march toward truth is any straighter today than a century ago, nor that we are closer to knowing how best to prevent disease. In the early 1900s a number of theories to account for the major diseases competed for attention. The hegemony of the miasma theory—just like the even more widespread acceptance, later, of the germ theory—was inextricably linked to nineteenth-century beliefs about the proper organization of society and, more fundamentally, to convictions about the nature of human beings. To know how the environmental approach to disease control came to dominate public health policy, and to help us understand current debates about the validity of such a perspective, we must look at the effects of political ideology on notions of disease causality.

In this chapter I describe four major nineteenth-century theories of disease causality, the preventive measures they demanded, and the political and economic beliefs with which they were associated. Although for the most part they were aimed at infectious diseases, they were, with one exception, remarkably similar to the theories advanced today to account for chronic ill-nesses. There was a contagion theory, similar to today's notion that germs cause disease; a personal behavior theory much like the current lifestyle theory; a miasma theory, the ancestor of our environmental approach; and—here is the exception—a super-natural theory. Before I turn to these beliefs about disease cau-sality, however, let me briefly sketch the picture of disease at the beginning of the Industrial Revolution.

Although population graphs indicate an overall steady fall in the European death rate beginning about 1770, nineteenth-century Europeans still faced sudden, uncontrollable epidemics which sent the death rate up again for short periods, principally in the growing urban slums. The most prevalent disease, an ail-ment responsible for as many as a third of all deaths in the early 1900s, was tuberculosis.[1] Other upper respiratory tract infec-tions killed almost as many people, followed by a variety of in-testinal infections.[2] Most of these diseases were accepted with a certain amount of forbearance (indeed, tuberculosis was roman-ticized) because their occurrence was interwoven with the ex-pected pattern of life. But few people were sanguine in face of the infamous epidemic diseases: typhus, cholera, plague, and yellow fever. These, because they came on so rapidly and caused death so quickly, give rise to mass terror and inspired demands that the government do something to prevent them.

Typhus had had a long history in Europe. First breaking out during a civil war in Spain in 1489, it accompanied virtually every European war and revolution for the next four hundred years.[3] In the late eighteenth century, it became a peacetime disease as well, taking up residence in the tenements surrounding the In-dustrial Revolution's new factories. There it began for the first time to claim the lives of urban dwellers in great numbers. Some historians assert that in 1848 typhus caused the deaths of four-teen out of every thousand people in England and Wales.[4] It was a major contender for the distinction of halting the long downward trend in the overall death rate, a trend which not only alarmingly leveled out at the beginning of the nineteenth century but for a short period reversed itself.[5]

Cholera, in contrast, was a new disease to most of the world in the nineteenth century. Unknown outside India before 1817, it suddenly broke whatever bonds had held it there and, on five separate occasions in the nineteenth century, swept across the globe. After the first outbreak in 1817, pandemics, lasting from six to twenty-two years, began in 1826, 1840, 1863, and 1883. Moscow and its suburbs had 8,431 cases and 4,588 deaths between September 1830 and January 1831.[6] The Scottish epidemic of 1832 killed nearly 10,000.[7] During carnival week that year in Paris, 5,523 people died from the disease.[8] And in 1849 cholera took 150,000 lives in France.[9] Şimilar tragedies occurred in the Americas, where cholera first appeared in 1832, and throughout Asia, the Near East, and Africa.

As for the plague, although it had been absent from Europe for a hundred years, people in the early 1800s still feared its return. In 1822, when the drowned body of the poet Shelley washed up on the shore of Tuscany, Italian authorities would not at first allow Shelley's friends access to it, so fearful were they that he might have died of plague.[10] Charles Creighton mentions a 1799 rumor of plague in London,[11] and the continued presence of the dread disease in the Middle East prompted a British navy surgeon to write in 1801, "To the list of the three contending powers in Egypt, France, Britain and Turkey must be added a fourth, bubonic plague, perhaps the most masterful belligerent of all."[12]

The fear that these three diseases inspired in Europe in the nineteenth century must have been heightened by the knowledge that virulent epidemics of yellow fever periodically swept the Americas and Africa. Yellow fever did not appear in Europe above the most southern regions of Spain and Portugal—nor has it ever infected Asia—but there was no rationale for this absence, and like plague, no one could say for sure that it would not come to Europe next. Epidemics of yellow fever took thousands of American lives during both the eighteenth and nineteenth centuries. For example, a tenth of the population of Philadelphia succumbed to yellow fever in 1793,[13] and five years later the disease killed 1,600 New Yorkers.[14] Americans are said to have feared it more than they did cholera.

Up until the nineteenth century, preventive measures against these diseases had been relatively noncontroversial. But with the social change accompanying industrialization, disease prevention began to acquire political meaning. No longer merely ways to control diseases, prevention policies became standard-bearers for the contending political arguments about the form the new society would take. Each effort to prevent disease was based on one or the other of four theories of disease causality. For the most part, the measures were centuries old, and because medical opinion held that all illnesses are manifestations of one disease, they applied indiscriminately to all cases of sickness.

CONTAGION THEORY

At the beginning of the nineteenth century, most official disease prevention activity was based, as it had been since the Black Death, on the hypothesis that illness is contagious. It required keeping sick people away from well people. The Venetians had instituted quarantine of ships during the Black Death,[15] and the practice of isolating vessels suspected of carrying infection continued throughout the subsequent plague epidemics. In some cases, ports were completely shut down; those on the Black Sea closed for two years during one plague epidemic.[16] But the traditional period was forty days ("la quarantina"), during which time ships, their crews, and cargoes waited offshore or at some isolated island.

On the land, isolating the sick from the well took similar forms. Local officials throughout the centuries set up military cordons around infected towns. Sometimes travelers could come and go as long as they showed no signs of illness, and other times entire cities and their environs were closed, either to keep disease in or to keep it out. When yellow fever struck Philadelphia in 1793, Baltimorians refused to let anyone into the city who had been in Philadelphia during the previous seven days, and other East Coast cities soon followed suit.[17] Later, in Russia, when cholera arrived, the authorities tried to protect Moscow by cutting off all roads to the city, and they extended the practice to other major cities around the country as the disease spread.[18] Isolation and quarantine also applied to physical objects like the suitcases and trunks of travelers, which were not only fumigated but in some instances kept at checkpoints for a week or more although their owners were free to continue their journeys.[19]

In addition to isolating towns from one another, officials in some cities quarantined houses in which anyone fell ill, prohibiting the entire household from leaving until the patient either recovered or died. In other places they searched out sick people and forced them into isolated hospitals. These practices were frequently as inhumane as they sound. During the cholera epidemics in Russia the police, charged with identifying and bringing in suspected patients, seized anyone who looked suspicious. So brutal were they that "no person was safe on the streets. The sick and cured well, the inebriates and the infirm were collared, dumped unceremoniously into the dreaded cholera carts, and hauled off willy-nilly into the lazarettes, often with whole families trailing the wagons weeping and wailing."[20]

What occurred within people's homes was harder to control, but official nineteenth-century rules in many cities mandated fumigating or washing the bedding and clothing of the sick. Like the idea that people carried disease, the idea that linens could become contaminated dated back hundreds of years. An Elizabethan plague bulletin, for example, warned that "noe Clothes, Linnen, or other like thing be hanged owt or over into the streete."[21] During the 1823–1832 cholera epidemic in Russia, people were ordered to wash their sick relatives' bed linens and clothing in brine or lye.[22] About the same time, the British Central Board of Health ruled that "goods" in the homes of the sick should be purified and burned.[23]

Personal practices—primarily avoiding other people—augmented official prevention measures. Chroniclers of epidemics often remarked on the accompanying breakdown in human intercourse. In his account of the Philadelphia yellow fever epidemic in 1793, Powell said, "People quickly acquired the habits of living with fear. Handshaking was abandoned, acquaintances snubbed, everyone walked in the middle of the streets to avoid contaminated houses. Those wearing mourning bands were obviously dangerous, as were doctors and ministers. People maneuvered in passing to get to windward of anyone they met."[24]

While some people simply kept their distance from others, for an unknown number the fear of contagion reached such heights that they abandoned even their own families when the signs of illness appeared. In *The Decameron*, Boccaccio laments that "brother forsook brother, uncle nephew and sister brother and ofttimes wife husband; nay (what is yet more extraordinary and well nigh incredible) fathers and mothers refused to visit or tend their very children, as they had not been theirs."[25] And a nineteenth-century U.S. Navy surgeon repudiated contagionism thus: "Humanity demands that the idea of contagion should be discountenanced . . . since it calls forth the worst features of the human heart, in its ungovernable terror, and frequently causes even the mother to desert her dying child, and the sick and friendless stranger to languish, uncared for and shunned."[26]

The contagion hypothesis was, throughout history, embellished by whatever xenophobic and prejudicial attitudes prevailed at the time. During the Black Death untold thousands of Jews were executed for their presumed role in causing the disease, perhaps as many as sixteen thousand in Strasbourg alone in 1349.[27] During subsequent plague epidemics, lepers, gravediggers, and supposed witches, as well as Jews, suffered derision, torture, expulsion, and often death for the same reason.[28] In Brazil a seventeenth-century yellow fever epidemic served as an excuse to constrain women; all prostitutes were sent away or jailed, and no upper-class women could leave their homes unless accompanied by their slaves, husbands, or parents.[29] When cholera first came to Russia a rumor circulated among the poor that the wealthy class had invented the disease as a new means of oppression; and doctors, especially foreign doctors, suspected of a role in disease transmission, risked physical violence as they moved from hospital to sickbed.[30] In England suspicion centered on the Irish, who were already considered the pests of society.[31] In India, of course, people blamed the English, while in Italy both the English and the French were held responsible.[32]

Sporadic scientific writings had bolstered the contagion theory for centuries by proposing methods by which disease could be transmitted among people. A number of sixteenth-century thinkers, the most notable being Girolamo Fracastoro in 1546, had suggested the existence of "contagium animulum." In the seventeenth century Anton van Leeuwenhoek actually observed bacteria and protozoa in his microscope (labeling them "little animals"). The eighteenth century produced a few more elaborations on what would eventually be known as the germ theory of disease, but the whole idea had already begun to lose adherents. By the time Jacob Henle wrote his now-famous description of the connection between illness and microorganisms in 1840, the contagion hypothesis was in such disrepute that only a handful of people paid attention. To most of his contemporaries, Henle was obsolete.[33]

Two problems confounded acceptance of the contagion hypothesis. First, it just did not account for enough. There were simply too many instances where people became ill regardless of their isolation from human contact and too many others where brave souls nursed the dying and carried their bodies to the graveyards yet remained well. In addition, while fugitives from an epidemic seemed to take disease with them, there were places to which epidemics never spread. Furthermore, the most dramatic attempts to test the contagion hypothesis often failed to support it. Dedicated physicians who tried to induce disease in themselves by experimentally ingesting the vomit or feces of the sick were frequently unsuccessful. They stayed healthy regardless.

The second problem with the contagion hypothesis was both political and economic: contagionism demanded quarantine, and in the nineteenth century, for the first time in history, quarantine became a critical political and economic issue. All during the plague epidemics of the Middle Ages and for long afterward, Europe was largely agricultural. Travel was infrequent and uncomfortable, for roads were muddy or dusty and full of ruts and unexpected holes. So insignificant was trade between most European communities that even extended quarantines affected only a handful of people; thus no major economic consequences followed on the concept that diseases are contagious. By the turn of the nineteenth century, however, all this had changed. In England, particularly, the Industrial Revolution was in full swing. Industrialists imported millions of pounds of raw cotton from India every year (the amount grew from 11 million pounds in 1785 to 588 million pounds in 1850)[34] and exported an ever-increasing number of yards of cotton cloth.[35] According to one historian, between 1842 and 1857 British exports increased by 130 percent.[36] Bristol and Liverpool became dependent on the infamous triangular trade in which manufacturers exported cotton goods and metalware to the Caribbean and North America for sugar, raw cotton, and tobacco, which were then imported into England. Roads, waterways, ports, and soon railroads gained central importance to the economy. For the new class of entrepreneurs and laborers building the new industrial society, quarantine spelled disaster.

Consequently, as Erwin Ackerknecht so ably demonstrates, disease causality ceased to be primarily a medical issue.[37] It was impossible to separate the scientific debate about disease causality from the economic consequences of its application. Contagionism meant closing ports. Hence the theory was opposed not only by the new industrialists, but by a vociferous group of politically liberal physicians who argued against contagionism on economic and political grounds. They made no bones about the economic implications of the disease causality argument. In fact, says Ackerknecht,

> Anticontagionists usually emphasized readily this popular aspect of the problem. They wrote long and detailed dissertations on exactly how many millions of pounds, francs, or dollars were

yearly lost through the contagionist error. Chervin [a leading French physician], who characterized the whole as a political, administrative, moral, medical, and commercial problem, was not afraid of such revealing word combinations as "question du plus haut intérêt pour l'humanité et le commerce" or "entraver le commerce et consacrer une erreur funeste à l'humanité." Gaultier wrote in 1833: "Quarantine is useless and the injury it inflicts on the commercial relations and maritime intercourse of the country is an absolute and uncompensated evil." Anticontagionist medical journals reprinted speeches of commerce-minded deputies. Liberal and commercial newspapers like the *Journal de Commerce*, the *Constitutionel*, and the *Courier* supported Chervin in 1827.[38]

In other words, to make their case, anticontagionist physicians dressed up contagionism in symbolic garb that linked it to the ancien régime. Contagionism, they implied, was the province of vapid mentalities, of people with no sense of progress, leftovers from the prescientific era who revered authority for its own sake. They called quarantines ineffective and charged that closing ports was mere mindless bureaucracy. In sum, they argued against contagionism on the grounds that it was inconsistent with the ideals of progress, individualism, and freedom that guided the Industrial Revolution.

This liberal ideology—the notion that the purpose of society is to progress; that people are basically competitive; and that if men are free from feudal obligations and bureaucratic interference, their competitive human nature will blossom and bring about progress—was so firmly believed by the new industrial class that it seemed an irrefutable truth, no more necessary of examination than the knowledge that the world is round. With liberalism as a basis, contagionism was unnatural. Thus, a major reason for the suppression (however short-lived) of the contagionist theory of disease causality was the ability of anticontagionists to connect it to a threatening economic policy and an outmoded political philosophy. It became nearly impossible to advocate contagionism without aligning oneself with what most people took to be stifling authoritarianism and economic decay.

SUPERNATURAL THEORY

The second belief about disease causality became similarly linked to authoritarianism, and like the contagionist theory, arguments over its validity were at the same time arguments about the proper organization of society. Proponents of this theory held that diseases are caused by supernatural forces. By today's standards this belief hardly warrants serious consideration among the more scientific nineteenth-century theories about diseases. Indeed, most medical historians ignore it. But disease prevention measures based on the theory were important to religious people—especially, in the early nineteenth century, in America—and like the other three contenders for official acceptance, the supernatural theory was as easily proved as disproved.

The notion that disease is supernatural in origin has a long history. In simple societies, people characteristically attribute disease to evil spirits, and the New Testament frequently refers to disease-causing demons. Such a belief in demonology makes disease a capricious event over which ordinary people have little control, and it limits prevention measures to ceremonial exorcism. Somewhat more reassuring, because it allows for preventive action, is the belief, expressed throughout the Old Testament, that disease comes not from the devil but from God. Being sick indicates a fall from grace. "When man came first out of the Hand of the Great Creator," wrote John Wesley, "cloth'd in Body as well as in Soul, with Immortality and Incorruption, there was no Place for Physick, or the Art of Healing. As he knew no Sin, so he knew no Pain, no Sickness, Weakness or Bodily Disorders."[39] Other religious people took the notion that illness is divine punishment to an extreme. During a 1721 smallpox outbreak, some Boston Puritans refused the new technique of variolation on the grounds that such disease prevention interfered with God's will.[40]

In the early nineteenth century most religious people at least partly accepted the view that disease is a punishment for transgression against God's laws. Therefore, when epidemics occurred, it behooved the whole society to pray, confessing their unworthiness, repenting of their sins, and humbly asking the Lord to spare them. Ministers in the United States commonly responded to epidemics by announcing fasts or holding prayer meetings.[41] Likewise, many Russian churches held special services to control cholera.[42] The following prayer written for Protestant Episcopal churches in New Orleans during that city's 1793 yellow fever epidemic illustrates the disease prevention measures exacted by the supernatural theory:

> Oh! Almighty and merciful God, to whom alone belong the issues of life and death, we, thy servants, bowed down under a deep sense of our unworthiness, do meekly acknowledge that we have grievously sinned, by thought, word and deed against thy Divine Majesty; and that by our sins we have most justly provoked thy wrath and indignation against us. . . . Spare us, good Lord, spare thy servants, who are grieved with remembrance of our sins, and turn from us the ravages of pestilence, wherewith, for our iniquities Thou art now visiting us. And mercifully grant that while this, Thy Fatherly correction, may teach us, ever, hereafter, to be mindful of Thy righteous judgment, it may also impress us, with a sense of our dependence upon Thee; lead us, now to put our whole trust and confidence in Thy mercy, and evermore to serve and please Thee, in newness of life, through Jesus Christ our Lord. Amen.[43]

Because epidemics took a greater toll on the poor than the rich, the healthier rich could employ the supernatural theory as a justification for berating the poor for sinful behavior: their presumed idleness, intemperance, and uncleanliness. The more self-righteous clergymen delivered thundering sermons denouncing sick sinners, and laymen wrote condemnatory letters to newspapers. One New York minister assured his flock that cholera, which first appeared in the slums, served to "promote the cause of righteousness by sweeping away the obdurate and incorrigible" and "to drain off the filth and scum which contaminates and defiles human society."[44] Employing the same metaphor, the editor of a Sunday school publication wrote, "Drunkards and filthy, wicked people of all descriptions, are swept away in heaps, as if the Holy God could no longer bear their wickedness. . . . The cholera is not caused by intemperance and filth in themselves, but it is a scourge in the hands of God."[45]

Other people found the supernatural theory of disease causality a handy way to castigate their enemies. For example, during the severe 1793 yellow fever epidemic in Philadelphia, both Republicans and Federalists blamed the immorality of the other party for bringing down God's wrath. And Republican clergymen, already angered over an ornate new theater being built downtown (the clergy opposed all forms of public gaiety, including dancing, card playing, and stage plays), charged that God's displeasure over the theater caused the suffering, pain, and death.[46]

These examples aside, only a few extremists accepted the supernatural theory as the sole explanation for disease; not many people, even among the very religious, argued that disease prevention required nothing more than prayer and piety. Sin was only a predisposing cause of disease. But even a partial acceptance of the theory implied a conservative political attitude because its adherents were overwhelmingly political conservatives. It should not be surprising, then, to learn that President Andrew Jackson refused to proclaim a national day of prayer to abate the 1832 cholera epidemic. Respect for the supernatural theory, or at least respect for its adherents, had prompted Presidents Washington, Adams, and Madison to proclaim fast days to combat disease, and some eleven governors announced official days of prayer to avert the 1832 cholera epidemic.[47] But Jackson could not follow their example. He cited separation of church and state as a rationale for his refusal, but the issue went deeper. The supernatural theory did not merely explain disease; it also addressed poverty.

Early nineteenth-century America was locked in a bitter political struggle over the values that would guide its future. On one side, the Jacksonians, the Democrats, the Freethinkers, the newly politicized members of the working class, and the anticlerical radicals argued for egalitarianism. Jackson's presidency meant at minimum a symbolic victory for these forces and gave new legitimacy to calls for political democracy, universal education, and the rights of the common man.[48] These slogans carried various meanings. For most people, egalitarianism never implied the transfer of wealth; poverty could be eliminated by simply providing equality of opportunity.[49] Others, political descendants of Tom Paine such as Frances Wright, Robert Dale Owen, and George Henry Evans, advanced economic theories that presaged Marx's. But whatever their place on the political spectrum, Jackson's supporters agreed that poverty sprang not from personal inadequacies but from economic conditions. Government, they believed, should redress the growing division between rich and poor. It followed that epidemics, most of which attacked the poor first, could no more be countered by prayer than could poverty itself be eliminated by church attendance and pious thoughts. Both the existence of poverty and the unequal distribution of disease were manifestations of the unjust political programs of Jackson's predecessors.

These notions contrasted vividly with the social ideas of those predecessors and their enduring supporters: the Whigs, the aristocracy, the clergy, and the remnants of the Federalists. Embracing authoritarianism and social hierarchy, the Whigs and their fellow conservatives argued for less democracy rather than more. "The distinction of rich and poor," wrote Noah Webster in 1837, "does exist and must always exist; no human power or device can prevent it." He argued against the popular election of presidents because "the great masses of people are and always must be very incompetent judges."[50]

The most powerful antidemocratic voice during this period came from the same people who preached that disease was caused by sin: the clergy, particularly the influential northern evangelists, who rarely hesitated to plunge into politics. Believing that God controlled the most minute earthly events and that political institutions were divinely inspired, they thought it evil to try to change government.[51] The Reverend Lyman Beecher wrote to a friend in 1812, "I am persuaded that the time has come when it behooves every friend of the state to wake up and exert his whole influence to save it from innovation and democracy."[52]

From this point of view, the supernatural theory of disease causality was both logical and politically necessary. It bolstered the notion that poverty can be explained by sin, and it warned Americans against the Jacksonian assumption that poverty can be alleviated by democracy. Thus the supernatural theory expressed more than a belief about disease. It also advanced a political philosophy. People could not advocate the belief that sin causes disease without at the same time implicitly supporting the idea that government need not redress poverty.

Personal Behavior Theory

In contrast to the supernatural theory of disease causality, the third major proposal held that disease results from wrong personal behavior. Democratic and antiauthoritarian in intent, it gave responsibility to individuals to control their own lives. In this formulation the source of disease was not tied up with the mysterious ways of God. Instead, people caused their own diseases by living unhealthfully. Improper diet, lack of exercise, poor hygiene, and emotional tension became the focus of preventive action. The personal behavior theory was entirely private. Far from asking for government support or sanctions, it rejected the help of all traditional disease prevention institutions.

The idea that diet, exercise, cleanliness, and emotions affect health has roots in classical Greek civilization, nourished in part by ancient convictions about the connection between mind and body. Its blossoming in the early nineteenth century attended that era's fascination with nature and its developing emphasis on personal freedom. Both in regard to government and to health, many nineteenth-century Americans and Europeans hoped to throw off ancient "artificial" strictures and to live in a manner consistent with natural law. For government that meant laissez-faire capitalism and the end of aristocracy; for health it meant preventing and curing illness without physicians and the medical panoply of treatments and drugs. In each case, advocates repudiated all things artificial; nature (or one's conception of it) would prevail.

Sylvester Graham, an American temperance lecturer inspired by a desire to save humankind, was the major advocate of dietary reform. At a time when the well-to-do consumed enormous quantities of lard, butter, starches, and pork, commonly eating three meats at every meal and rarely touching vegetables, Graham campaigned for a "natural" low-sugar, low-fat diet, high in whole wheat products and vegetables and devoid of meat. He concocted the crackers that still bear his name and developed a special whole wheat bread. His passion for dietary change expanded into a crusade for bathing, exercise, fresh air, and "sex hygiene."[53] He edited a widely distributed health journal and lectured indefatigably all over the country, becoming well enough known to acquire a nickname: newsmen dubbed him "The Peristaltic Persuader."[54]

Graham's insistence that people could maintain their health without the "unnatural" medications and overbearing authority of doctors paled in comparison to the antidoctor position of Samuel Thomson. Thomson, a New Hampshire farmer turned herbalist, strongly appealed to the antiauthoritarian ideology of America's early nineteenth century. Promising people that by subscribing (for twenty dollars) to his botanical secrets, they would be forever free from doctors and apothecaries, he sold some one hundred thousand "Family Rights" to his practice between 1806 and 1840. The subscription included a sixteen-page booklet with herbal recipes, and the right to receive botanical journals, attend lectures, and correspond with other Thomson followers. The Thomsonian slogan, "Every man his own doctor," with its overtones of self-reliance, attracted subscribers from all classes.[55] Or at least it attracted people who could afford, in the 1830s, to spend twenty dollars on a book.

A third antidoctor, pronature fancy was that water could cure and prevent disease, and throughout the nineteenth century, in Europe and the United States, men and women with money staked their health on water cures. At first this "natural" way to health was limited to hydropathy, a medical concept countering the popular fear that getting wet all over was dangerous. Hydropaths encouraged their ailing—or worried—patients to attend mineral springs where they could soak in special baths, immerse themselves in hot mud, wrap their bodies in wet sheets, consume doses of mineral water, and expose themselves to restorative sprays, showers, and steams. Health journals devoted to hydropathy reported cures for everything from anemia, gout, and rheumatism to kidney stones, heart disorders, and "women's ailments." Although some doctors and other healers administered forms of water cure in patients' homes (pouring pitchers of water over their heads, for example), most hydropathy took place in spas. As one might suspect, spas tended to serve the wealthy and fashionable. Because the treatment was prolonged, patients brought their spouses, children, and personal servants, and eventually the daily regimen for the sick was embellished by boating, fishing, dancing, and sports for the well who accompanied them. By the end of the century most spas had become elegant vacation resorts complete, in some places, with full orchestras to entertain the guests, dozens of gardeners to maintain the grounds, and luxurious restaurants.[56]

Even at the beginning of the century, the equation of health with nature had little relevance for the poor. To suggest to a textile worker in 1830 that her health depended entirely on changing her diet (when she barely had money to buy the cheapest foods), on access to copious amounts of water (when she hauled hers from a distant pump), or on her ability to relax in warm sunshine (when stress and overwork in crowded slums defined her life) was certainly obtuse and probably useless. Nevertheless, advocates of this theory of disease causality proclaimed its virtues to everyone.

"The true means to preserve the natural tone of the body," airily wrote Noah Webster in 1799 in his enormously influential *History of Epidemic and Pestilential Disease* "are the most natural means."[57] He then went on to counsel eating just the right amount of food: "Too much produces unusual excitement, which is followed by indirect debility, a state of body which invites an attack of pestilence. Too little nourishment, on the other hand, induces direct debility, a state equally favorable to disease."[58] He warned against excessive sunshine—"Nothing is more dangerous than the burning heat of the sun"[59]—and physical exertion—"Labor should not be violent, and walking moderate."[60] He also preached that an easy supply of water is important for maintaining health: "Fresh water, frequently applied to the body receives and carries off all matter of infection, thus removing *one* copious source of the disease."[61]

Other popular medical books also ignored class disparities. The author of *Gunn's New Family Physician,* who echoed Webster's views about the importance of mental tranquility, gentle exercise, regular habits, and cleanliness, offered to laborers the same advice he gave to the upper classes: "Taylors, sawyers, shoemakers, engravers, watchmakers, and many others such as cotton-spinners, dress-makers present either awkward movements in limbs or eyes, or are sickly or sallow-looking. Such parties are commonly affected with indigestion, giddiness, headaches or diarrhea. . . . [T]here is no remedy for the evils referred to, but taking as much bodily exercise and outdoor recreation as possible."[62]

The personal behavior theory resembled the supernatural theory in making disease a personal event, not a political phenomenon requiring government action. But where the supernatural theory blamed sin for illness, the personal behavior theory pointed to inadequate health education and bad habits. The theory not so much blamed the poor for their illnesses as ignored poverty altogether. In many respects it was a homage to middle-class life. It extolled temperate behavior, controlled emotions, minimal physical labor, and the possession of enough money to allow for economic choices.

This proposal—that middle-class life best secured health—signified, in the absence of a call for economic reform, that the social order was good. It assumed that everyone already had the wherewithal to comply with the behavioral requirements for a healthy life. In some respects it thus served to support the economic status quo. But it also advanced the central political idea of modern times: the belief in individual freedom and autonomy. It denied the legitimacy of medical authority and underscored the liberating insistence that individuals should have the power to control their own lives.

MIASMA THEORY

The fourth major theory of disease causality, the miasma theory, contrasted sharply with the other three because it conceptually separated the source of disease from the victims of disease. This proposal dated back to the Hippocratic idea that disease is related to climate:

> Whoever wishes to investigate medicine properly, should proceed thus: in the first place to consider the seasons of the year, and what effects each of them produces. . . . Then the winds, the hot and the cold, especially such as are common to all countries, and then such as are peculiar to each locality. We must also consider the qualities of the waters, for as they differ from one another in taste and weight, so also do they differ much in their qualities. In the same manner, when one comes into a city to which he is a stranger, he ought to consider its situation, how it lies as to the winds and the rising sun; for its influence is not the same whether it lies to the north or the south, to the rising or to the setting sun.[63]

From this beginning, the relation between disease and weather was a matter of common sense as well as a subject for learned scholarship for nineteen centuries. Observations about the weather—drought, or an especially long winter or a cold spring, or an unusually warm autumn—commonly accompanied descriptions of epidemics from Greek times onward.

The connection between the atmosphere and disease was subject, in the nineteenth century, to a number of interpretations. Many believed that the air becomes pestilential or "corrupted" by earthquakes, tidal waves, blazing comets, thunder and lightning, great storms, or volcanic eruptions. Others were more apt to agree with Thomas Sydenham "that there are many Constitutions of Years that arise neither from Heat nor Cold nor Moisture nor Drought, but proceed from a secret and inexplicable alteration in the Bowels of the Earth whereby the Air is contaminated with such *effluvia* as dispose Bodies to this or that Disease."[64] Whether pestilential air was caused by typhoons or seasonal changes or elusive atmospheric shifts, this theory of disease causality left people helpless to prevent illness; it was much like believing in demonology. One's main recourse was to fumigate the air after it had become infected.

Three basic methods of fumigation evolved. In the first, people lit great bonfires in the city streets. Hippocrates is said to have ordered the burning of fragrant leaves, flowers, and ointments during epidemics,[65] and the practice continued into the nineteenth century. Reports of epidemics often contain accounts of aromatic bonfires burning in town squares or at the intersections of streets. Eventually someone thought of burning not-so-fragrant substances, presumably because fierce diseases might respond better. During the 1853 yellow fever epidemic in New Orleans, for example, frantic officials burned barrels of tar throughout the city and at the cemeteries, filling the air with such thick clouds of heavy, black smoke that the city is said to have resembled a northern manufacturing center.[66]

Shooting artillery or firing cannons constituted a second method of fumigation. It was believed to work "because the violence of the [artillery] fire is like a famished beast that by running wild disperses everything."[67] Third, people took personal precautions to keep the air immediately around them pure, using sweet-smelling oils (eau de cologne could ward off the plague) and less pleasant articles (onions, for example, or dead toads). Powell says that in Philadelphia those who dared to walk abroad during the 1793 fellow fever epidemics carried "tarred ropes or camphor bags and chewed garlic constantly, doused themselves with vinegar, carried smelling bottles or smoked tobacco. They emitted a curious odor for several yards. Even women and small boys . . . had segars almost constantly in their mouths."[68]

Not all ideas about pestilential air admitted only post hoc disease prevention. The atmospheric theory of disease contained within it another concept, one that identified man-made sources of disease. This idea traced the pestilential air not to uncontrollable meteorological or seasonal conditions but to miasmas: the foul odors that emanated from putrifying dead bodies (both animal and human), decomposing garbage, rank slaughterhouse offal, and fetid human wastes. Proponents of the miasma theory believed in the danger of smell itself. The air rising from or blowing across decaying organic matter was thought to be injurious to the body and dangerous to inhale, a conception similar to the present-day understanding that radioactive air or air laden with asbestos particles is harmful. In 1846 Southwood Smith explained the mechanism thus:

> Wherever animal and vegetable substances are undergoing the process of decomposition, poisonous matters are evolved which, mixing with the air, corrupt it, and render it injurious to health and fatal to life. . . . If provision is not made for the immediate removal of these poisons, they are carried by the air inspired to the air-cells of the lungs, the thin delicate membranes of which they pierce, and thus pass directly into the current of the circulation. It has been shown that by the natural and ordinary flow of this current, three distinct and fresh portions of these poisons must necessarily be transmitted to every nook and corner of the system in every eight minutes of time.[69]

The theory prescribed cleaning streets of garbage, burying the dead very deeply (during some epidemics the city burial places, crowded to their limits with hastily dug shallow graves, gave off nauseating odors), ventilating crowded rooms, and controlling the air arising from cesspools, privies, and sewers.

No one could deny that disgusting smells accompanied the Industrial Revolution. To house the flow of people pouring into the cities, unscrupulous builders erected slapdash dwellings around factories where people were packed together in appalling conditions. There was no sewage system, and in some English cities, as many as one hundred people shared a single privy.[70] Not infrequently, houses were built back to back, a practice which prevented the passage of air through rooms and left unpaved streets in front as the most convenient place to discard cooking slops and human wastes. Backyards and side lanes, where they existed, became thick with filth.

Proponents of the miasma theory argued their case with descriptions of shocking living conditions among the disease-ridden poor. Probably the most important was the 1842 *Report on the Sanitary Condition of the Labouring Population of Great Britain*, written by Edwin Chadwick, the secretary of Britain's Poor Law Commission. Implying throughout that foul odors cause diseases, the report serves as an excellent example of such arguments:

> Shepherd's Buildings consist of two rows of houses . . . placed back to back. There are no yards or out-conveniences; the privies are in the centre of each row. . . . The street between the two rows is seven yards wide, in the centre of which is the common gutter, or more properly sink, into which all sorts of refuse is thrown; it is a foot in depth. Thus there is always a quantity of putrefying matter contaminating the air. At the end of the rows is a pool of water very shallow and stagnant, and a few yards further, a part of the town's gas works. In many of these dwellings there are four persons in one bed.[71]

> From the absence of drains and sewers, there are of course few cellars entirely free from damp; many of those in low situations are literally inundated after a fall of rain. . . . Nor is this the full extent of the evil; the fluid matter of the court privies sometimes oozes through into the adjoining cellars, rendering them uninhabitable by any one whose olfactories retain the slightest sensibility. In one cellar in Lace-street I was told that the filthy water thus collected measured not less than two feet in depth; and in another cellar a well, four feet deep, into which this stinking fluid was allowed to drain, was discovered below the bed where the family slept![72]

> The filth of the gaol, containing on an average 65 prisoners, is floated down the public streets every second or third day, and emits, during the whole of its progress . . . the most offensive and

disgusting odour. The slaughter-house is situated near the top of
the town, and the blood from it is allowed to flow down the public
streets. The lower part of a dwelling-house, not more than three
or four yards from the town-house and gaol, is used as a "mid-
ding" and pigsty, the filth being thrown into it by window and
door. There are no public necessaries; and the common stairs
and closes, and even the public streets, are used habitually as
such, by certain classes of the community. Two drains from the
castle, convey the whole filth of it into an open field, where it
spreads itself over the surface, and pollutes the atmosphere to a
very great extent.[73]

The sanitary report recommended massive reforms. Chadwick believed disease could be prevented with a sewage system
capable of carrying household wastes and their odors away from
the city. He also wanted improved supplies of water.[74] At the
time he wrote, cities had drains for runoff from the street, but
they were not connected to houses (in fact, hookups were for-
bidden), and their brick construction, right angles, and irregular
slope frequently turned them into cesspools. Additionally, the
water companies only supplied water at centrally located pumps
on certain days at certain hours. To prevent disease, Chadwick
proposed piping water to every home, connecting each house to
the sewers, and redesigning sewers, shaping them like the cross
section of an egg to force water at high pressure continually
through the system. His plan called for a single administration
to take over from the decentralized, fragmented authority then
responsible for house drainage, street sewerage, water supply,
land drainage, and road structure.[75]

The publication of the sanitary report was a major event in a
ten-year struggle to win support in Parliament for an environmental approach to disease control. Lesser reports had preceded it, and an extensive lobbying campaign of public forums
and pamphleteering followed it. Despite the fact that it raised
the ire of large numbers of influential people, including physicians championing contagion theory, the owners of water companies, the exponents of local government, and the editors of
the *Times*,[76] it culminated in the Public Health Act of 1848, giv-

ing official sanction to the miasma theory of disease and laying the foundations for the famous sanitary "revolution" of the nineteenth century.

The hegemony of the miasma theory can be explained by the political meaning it acquired: its proponents linked it to the virtues of individualism. Like the personal behavior theory of disease causality, disease prevention based on the miasma theory would be consistent with the values of self-sufficiency and individual autonomy. But the miasma theory, requiring government initiatives, went beyond that. The policies it implied would repudiate the ancien régime's reliance on tradition and sentiment as guides for action. Instead they would advance the pragmatic values of efficiency, thrift, and self-interest. The miasma theory spoke to the utilitarian calculus that judged all government action according to whether it expedited industrial production. Adherents of the miasma theory argued that while spending to clean up the urban environment might appear to increase the sphere of government, the cleanup would actually lessen the need for bureaucracies devoted to other problems. The most forceful among these adherents was Edwin Chadwick, the author of the *Report on the Sanitary Condition*. A disciple of Jeremy Bentham, Chadwick had been responsible for the creation of the Poor Law Commission, and his ideas formed the substance of the New Poor Law, the regulations which, by cutting the amount the government spent on the poor to less than a person could earn, forced people to the cities, reduced wages, and created a new labor market. His turning to public health was an extension of the twin concerns that had led him to study poverty: that people needed to stand on their own two feet and that the government spent too much money on poor relief. He hoped both to reduce the number of state-supported widows and orphans, by reducing the death rate among the working class, and to increase production among those who did work. It was as straightforward as that, and the report appealed to its readers on exactly those grounds.[77]

After describing in detail the unsanitary conditions in which the working class lived, Chadwick underscored the class nature of the problem. He compared the mortality rate among "gentlemen and persons engaged in the professions and their families" with the rate for tradesmen and farmers and the rate for laborers, operative mechanics, and servants. He then devoted about half the report to an attempt to assign a cost to diseases and death. Some of the cost is to laborers, he wrote, because of their loss of "healthful existence and happiness."[78] The rest is cost to employers in the form of lost profits and to the community in the forms of lost produce and "expenditure for the relief of destitution, which original cost (the bad ventilation) we have high scientific authority for stating to be easily and economically controllable."[79] In other words, spending now to get rid of foul odors would save money in the long run.

He was as specific as possible, estimating on the basis of samples that "nearly 27,000 cases of premature widowhood, and more than 100,000 cases of orphanage may be ascribed to removable causes."[80] He pointed out long-term consequences of orphanhood. Widows infrequently remarry, he said; they raise all their children on state money, and when the children grow up, "the early familiarity with the parochial relief makes them improvident and they fall back upon the poor's rates on the lying-in of their wives, on their sickness, and for aid in every emergency."[81]

He showed that not only were homes unhealthy but so were factories and mines. He urged that they too should be cleaned up, since "the average period of the working ability of that class might be extended at least ten years by improvements as to the places of work alone."[82] He also tried to demonstrate that bad character is caused by living in filth (instead of the other way around, as the behavior and supernatural theorists believed). People living in squalor, he claimed, become "improvident, reckless, and intemperate, and with habitual avidity for sensual gratifications."[83] He supported these claims by including letters from local officials. One official, for example, wrote that without decent housing, people "spend their earnings weekly in the beer shop; associating with the worst of characters, they become the worst of labourers, resort to poaching, commit petty thefts, and add to the county rates by commitments and prosecutions."[84] In the concluding chapter, Chadwick reiterated his finding that the "noxious influences in place of work and abode" cut an average of eight to ten years "of work ability" from the laboring class, and he reminded his readers that public loss from these premature deaths is greater than would be the "pecuniary burden" of preventing them.

As the basis for the campaign for the sanitary report, the argument for the miasma theory thus became simultaneously an argument for fiscal prudence. Providing sewerage and clean water was not linked just to disease prevention; it also meant saving money for the taxpayers and assuring a more productive work force for the industrialists. More important, people saw frugality and efficiency as admirable (instead of, say, stingy and heartless) because these goals expressed values at the heart of nineteenth-century individualism. They advanced self-fulfillment and freedom from authority. They meant limited government and social progress. Because these values appealed so strongly to the most politically powerful groups in the new society, the miasma theory came to predominate over all others. And the disease prevention policies it engendered worked. A focus on the general environment instead of on particular agents of disease, personal behavior, or relation to God dramatically reduced the incidence of infectious disease. The question now is, Would a similar policy today reduce chronic diseases, and if so, what constrains us from putting it into place?

CHAPTER 2

Twentieth-Century Debates

One might imagine that, although economic and ideological considerations influenced nineteenth-century disease prevention policy, sound research determines policy today. Certainly current wisdom has it that in the twentieth century the growth of science rescues debate about disease causality from the politicians. Unlike their ancestors a hundred years ago, policy makers can, in the face of chronic diseases, look to science to provide apolitical facts on which to base preventive action. While we are a long way from actually eradicating cardiovascular disease and cancer, at least there is a reliable source of unbiased information about their causes.

Unfortunately, current wisdom errs. The three theories of disease causality that confront policy makers today have each acquired a political meaning. As a result, scientific arguments for and against them mask new versions of the same political arguments that challenged our ancestors a century ago. But this time, ironically, progress is associated with the idea that microorganisms cause disease, while economic stagnation is linked to the belief that the air, water, and soil are dangerous.

Most people in the United States and other industrialized countries die today from heart disease. It claims about 32 percent of the population. Cancer, despite the fear it engenders, takes substantially fewer lives—about 24 percent. The third and fourth major causes of death are stroke and violence, but they are each responsible for only about 6 percent of mortality. If we break down death rates according to age and look just at people between fifteen and thirty-four, violence (accidents, homicide, and suicide) becomes by far the most common cause of death. But our interest here in chronic diseases and their prevention makes distribution according to social class more salient than distribution according to age.

Social class is a slippery concept, an abstraction, ascertainable only through its indicators. But almost every study that has attempted to correlate mortality with social class, regardless of how it defined social class, has found an inverse relation between the two. People with the least education, people who live in the least desirable neighborhoods, and people who work at the least prestigious jobs are all more likely to die earlier than people on the other end of these scales.[2] Data published every decade by the British Office of Population and Censuses provide the best documentation. Figure 1 shows that virtually every disease strikes the lowest class most heavily. This is not a new finding; it goes back to the early nineteenth century when such studies were first made.[3] Its basic lesson, many people say, is that disease is caused by environmental factors. Counterclaims that these statistics merely reflect unequal medical care, that they are an artifact of previous but now-addressed inequalities, or that they confuse cause with effect are inconsistent with the most recent data.[4] More controversial is the definition of "environmental factors." Exactly what these factors are, what sort of disease prevention policies they call for, what the chances are that an environmental theory of disease causality will predominate again—these are the questions I discuss in this chapter. They can be best answered by comparing today's environmental theory with the germ and lifestyle theories that oppose it.

GERM THEORY

Near the end of the nineteenth century, the germ theory, reviled as obsolete by enthusiasts of the miasma proposal, made a

Fig. 1. Mortality by Social Class and Cause of Death: Standardized Mortality Rates for Men and Married Women (by Husband's Occupation) Aged 15–64

KEY:
Black bars: Men
Hatched bars: Married Women
I   Professional occupations
II   Intermediate occupations
III_N   Skilled nonmanual occupations
III_M   Skilled manual occupations
IV   Partly skilled occupations
V   Unskilled occupations

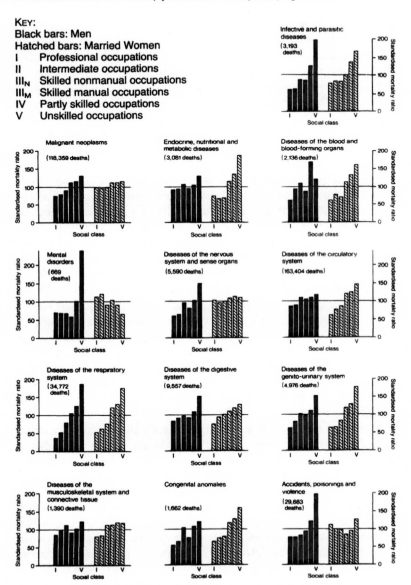

SOURCE: Great Britain, Office of Population Censuses and Surveys, *Occupational Mortality*, 1970–1972 (London: HMSO, 1978), 41.

spectacular comeback. Carrying with it this time the possibility of antibiotics and vaccines to control diseases without the threat of quarantine, the theory rapidly overtook other explanations for disease. It promised to explain all illnesses, holding out hope for a disease-free world. At first applied only to what we now call infectious disease, by the turn of the twentieth century, the germ theory had prompted scientists to search for a microorganism that can cause cancer. The pursuit concentrated on viruses. In 1911 Peyton Rous, working with chickens at the Rockefeller Institute, produced the first clear demonstration that viruses are implicated in malignant tumor formation. The discovery won him a Nobel Prize in 1966. In 1933 Richard Shope, also at the Rockefeller Institute, isolated an oncogenic (or tumor-causing) virus in rats with breast cancer. The excitement these discoveries generated (these and other researchers published some fifty papers on cancer viruses between 1911 and 1940) died down during the Second World War, but in the early 1950s the search for cancer viruses picked up again. A new generation of scientists has now published hundreds of papers linking viruses to cancers in mice, rabbits, guinea pigs, monkeys, hamsters, and frogs as well as in chickens and rats. In 1972 the U.S. government declared a "war on cancer," lavishly funding investigations primarily based on the viral theory. The hope, of course, is that the pursuit of cancer viruses will eventually result in the development of a vaccine, thus ending the fear of cancer so prevalent in the United States today.

Disputes. The missing link in the germ theory of cancer causality is the positive identification of a human cancer virus. Despite all the research, no one has yet isolated a virus that can unequivocally be said to cause cancer in humans. Animal data only tells us about animals. It cannot automatically be applied to human populations. Indeed even some animal cancer viruses are known to be mere laboratory artifacts, events that only occur in the artificial conditions created in the laboratory.[5] Interest in a viral cancer theory will undoubtedly continue to fluctuate, but most scientists today tend to respond skeptically to claims that viruses acting alone can cause cancer in humans. Everyone agrees that some viruses have been *correlated* with human cancer; it is their causal relation that scientists debate.[6] Debate centers on five viruses: (1) Epstein-Barr virus, which is linked to Burkitt's lymphoma, a cancer endemic in some parts of tropical Africa, and to nasopharyngeal carcinoma, a common cancer in Asia; (2) herpes simplex virus type 2, which is associated with cancer of the cervix; (3) papilloma virus, also connected to cervical cancer, as well as to bowel cancer; (4) hepatitis B virus, implicated in hepatocellular carcinoma, a liver cancer rare in the United States but important in the third world; and (5) human T-cell lymphocyte virus (called HTLV), which has been recovered from leukemia patients in the United States and Japan.[7]

At issue is whether these viruses are able to cause cancer by themselves. Epstein-Barr virus, for example, is common all over the world, but Burkitt's lymphoma occurs only in malarious areas of tropical Africa, not even in other tropical places with malaria. Similarly, epidemiologic studies show not just a link between herpes type 2 virus and cervical cancer but also a link among the virus, sexual behavior, and poverty.[8] Such information confounds the hypothesis that viruses alone can cause human cancer and buttresses the conviction held by many critics of medicine that the germ theory is too narrow a basis either for disease prevention policy or for effective medical care. The critics argue their case from the historical record.

Political implications. During the remarkable period of medical discoveries that began with the positive identification of disease-causing microbes, a host of virulent diseases, as well as many milder ones, were classified as infectious, that is, caused by microorganisms. The identification of particular microorganisms linked to specific diseases has made it possible to develop means of supplying the body with defenses against their invasion. In some cases, predominantly with viruses, this has meant injecting people with a vaccine that causes cells to manufacture antibodies against a specific microbe. In other cases, classically with bacteria, substances such as antibiotics have been developed to destroy a microorganism once it has begun to grow inside the body. So dramatic are these techniques that most people, including most physicians, give them credit for the freedom from infectious disease we know in industrial countries today.

The credit, however, is undeserved, for in Europe and North America the incidence of virtually all major infectious diseases began to fall several decades before the introduction of vaccines and antibiotics. Thomas McKeown, whose careful studies of disease records in the eighteenth and nineteenth centuries uncovered much supporting evidence for this realization, maintains that a rising standard of living, not the discoveries of bacteria and viruses, was responsible for the reduction of disease.[9] If this is true, the germ theory's current high status is based on questionable assumptions. It appears that social and political events that affect the standard of living, rather than microorganisms, are the salient determinants of health and disease and that disease causality is far more complex than the germ theory implies.[10] Certainly the blurry relation between oncogenic viruses and human cancer supports this conclusion. But the conclusion also holds for infectious diseases despite the unquestionable fact that preventive and curative medicine as well as disease prevention have benefited from the identification of microorganisms.

Doubts about the salience of the germ theory have so far had little effect on its currency. The theory has tremendous appeal in general, and even its critics do not advocate abandoning cancer virus research. But just as in the nineteenth century, it is hard to separate the theory that disease is caused by microorganisms from the theory's political implications.

The germ theory is virtually synonymous with science. It evokes images of white coats, sophisticated laboratories, dedicated researchers, and the relentless search for truth. Our society awards considerable prestige to people who investigate disease causality from the perspective of the germ theory. Because their attention is fixed on empirical phenomena, they are "real" scientists. Moreover, they employ methods too intricate for nonscientists to understand. The special language they speak heightens their prestige. When they talk about their work with the general public, they must translate into ordinary terms the words and phrases with which they communicate among themselves. By locating the cause of disease in a microorganism, they keep the problem of disease prevention in the laboratory. From this perspective, health is a technical problem, not a social problem, and however complex chronic disease causality may now appear, scientists will eventually expose its seeming mystery.[11] In contrast, the scientists who concentrate on other disease hypotheses not only command less social prestige, but the methods of disease prevention their theories imply call for personal change and economic upheaval. This fact alone goes a long way toward explaining the appeal of the germ theory.

It is satisfying for policy makers to think of disease in the individualistic terms called up by the idea that microorganisms cause disease. They can view diseases as personal problems and conceive of disease prevention as the responsibility of the medical profession. In the case of cancer, if causal viruses are identified and vaccines developed, as many hope, cancer prevention would be synonymous with preventive medicine. Considering the alternatives, this is a heartening vision of the future. It allows policy makers justifiably to ignore people's complicated interaction with their social and physical environments, for it means that the *real* cause of disease, the fundamental cause, is tangible, identifiable, and individual.[12] Beyond that, and with particular significance for disease prevention policy, the germ theory sets up a causal chain, with microevents within the human body as the immediate cause of disease, personal behavior such as diet and exercise as intermediate causes, and environmental pollution as a tertiary cause. Sociopolitical realities such as poverty lie at the very end of the chain.

This conceptualization is familiar. It makes logical the idea that the most efficient method of disease prevention provides the individual human body with a way to fight invasions of microscopic particles, and it expands to advocate behavioral change only when no such particles have been identified. Changing the physical environment is, from this perspective, a third choice, and to attack poverty as a way to reduce disease becomes a last resort. Indeed, despite the discoveries of McKeown and his followers and despite the ancient inverse relation between social class and disease, most people cling to the germ theory as the real explanation for illness.

Ironically, the very lack of sensitivity to the context in which disease occurs also constitutes one of the germ theory's virtues. It makes disease impersonal. Concentrating on a causal microorganism helps guard against assigning responsibility for disease to the sick person's personal characteristics. During the plague epidemics, for example, Jews, foreigners, and other stereotyped groups would have suffered less vilification had the etiologic agent been identified. At the very least, there would have been a rationale besides benevolence for chastising xenophobes who used disease as a new excuse to abuse people. The homophobic response to AIDS today demonstrates the limits of that reasoning, for large sectors of the American public persist in believing that AIDS is caused by promiscuity, but the response surely would be far worse had no virus been isolated. By the same token, the focus of medicine on the diseased organ instead of on the sick patient has the virtue of urging physicians to treat all patients equally. Despite its negative social and emotional consequences (despite, that is, the way it can turn people into objects), this reductionist view of disease does discourage doctors from wondering whether their patients are personally worth their while.

LIFESTYLE THEORY

The second current hypothesis about disease causality holds that cardiovascular disease and cancer are caused by an unhealthy lifestyle. It shifts to the forefront the personal behavior factors, which from the perspective of the germ theory are only secondary contributors to disease. This hypothesis blames stress, lack of exercise, the use of alcohol and tobacco, and improper nutrition for most chronic disease. Lifestyle theorists reject the notion, central to the classic germ theory, that a single disease has a single etiology. Instead, they emphasize the interrelatedness of many variables in disease causality, principally those under the control of the individual. Nevertheless, this approach to disease resembles the germ theory, for it conceives of disease as an individual event. The difference is that prevention, instead of requiring physicians' ministrations, demands personal behavior change.

In the United States today, probably the most influential proponent of the lifestyle hypothesis is the U.S. Department of Health and Human Services. The surgeon general's much-quoted 1979 report on health promotion and disease prevention, *Healthy People*, embodies the message. Besides visiting your doctor regularly, the main actions you can take to keep healthy are to stop smoking, avoid misusing alcohol and drugs, improve your nutrition, exercise to keep fit, and reduce stress.[13] Americans had already worried about their health throughout the 1970s; long before this report came out, newspaper and magazine articles, industry advertisements, pamphlets in doctor's offices, lectures, television programs, and books were already bombarding Americans with the same news: your lifestyle is making you sick.

A major portion of the message concerns nutrition. Since 1961 the American Heart Association has recommended a "prudent" low-fat, low-cholesterol diet to reduce heart disease. In 1979 Arthur Upton, then head of the National Cancer Institute, announced that a diet high in fat and cholesterol also plays a role in cancer causation.[14] In 1982 at the request of the National Cancer Institute, the National Academy of Sciences convened a special panel, which extended the low-fat, low-cholesterol diet to include generous amounts of fresh fruits, vegetables, and whole grains. It recommended reduced salt and moderate amounts of alcohol.[15] In 1983 the American Cancer Society endorsed virtually the same diet, and in 1984 so did the National Cancer Institute and the National Institutes of Health.[16]

A second portion of the lifestyle hypothesis concerns stress. Some scientists consider stress an intermediate factor in disease and expect that its reduction can, as one physician put it, "free energy needed by the defense and immune system to eliminate cancer cells and permit exhausted adrenal glands to return to their normal function."[17] Others, uncertain about a causal relation between stress and disease, emphasize their association: "The onset of illness, both physical and psychiatric, has been shown to be preceded by a significant increase in stress."[18] Still others claim that stress can be the direct cause of illness. Hans Selye, the father of stress research, says, "Exposure to a variety of stressors can induce malignant growths, especially in predisposed species under certain conditions."[19]

Closely related to a concern with stress is the belief that sedentary living causes disease. To help people become more active, as well as teach them how to reduce tension and eat differently, "wellness clinics" and "fitness centers" now dot the country, and the more progressive corporations increasingly provide health programs for employees. Here, in gyms and converted meeting rooms, men and women exercise under supervision. The most elaborate programs employ physicians, psychologists, nutritionists, and exercise therapists to guide their clients in behavioral and dietary change.[20]

The best known component of the lifestyle theory is cigarette smoking. Epidemiologic studies have, since the 1950s, linked smoking to lung cancer and more recently to cancers of the mouth, larynx, esophagus, pancreas, kidneys, and bladder. The Department of Health and Human Services calls cigarette smoking the major single cause of cancer mortality in the United States, responsible for 30 percent of all cancer deaths, a figure translatable into premature death for 129,000 people.[21] Even more important, cigarette smoking is the major risk factor in coronary heart disease, responsible for an estimated 170,000 deaths per year.[22]

Disputes. A variety of arguments assail the notion that an unhealthful lifestyle accounts for disease. First, the role of diet in disease causality is, at best, contested. Much of the evidence that implicates diet in human cancer comes from epidemiologic studies that try to account for the large differences in cancer incidence between countries. Unfortunately, countries with high rates of cancer are distinguished from countries with low rates in many ways besides diet. It is extremely difficult to separate out the many factors that could possibly account for international mortality differences. Data from randomized trials are equally debatable. Even with the most careful selection of subjects, the most detailed questionnaires, and the most conscientious accounts of dietary habits, reliable information is hard to obtain. The trials must go on for a tediously long time and compliance inevitably declines; people in control groups as well as in case groups change their behavior; and recall by subjects is notoriously inaccurate.[23] For such reasons, the actual relation between chronic diseases and diet is not at all clear.

Take, for example, the role that cholesterol plays in disease. Whereas people with heart disease have, as a group, high levels of blood cholesterol, it is not at all clear that decreasing cholesterol in the diet saves lives. Moreover, new evidence suggests that lowered cholesterol levels may actually be dangerous for some people.[24] In addition, although evidence that carotene and vitamins A, C, and E may prevent cancer prompts many scientists to recommend a diet of fresh fruits and vegetables, a 1985 panel appointed by the National Academy of Sciences was unable to agree on guidelines for optimal intake of vitamins and minerals.[25] One British study even found an inverse relation between vitamin A and lung cancer.[26] Similarly, recent studies question the causal relation between dietary fiber and disease,[27] and between salt and disease.[28] The National Academy of Sciences has been particularly skeptical of the health claims for dietary fiber.[29]

A 1984 review article on the diet issue in the *New England Journal of Medicine* concludes that the evidence for a diet-cancer link is weak. The authors cheerfully remark, however, that the recommended diets "seem sensible, not so much because of the firmness of any expectation that cancer rates will be lowered by such actions, but because the changes are unlikely to be harmful and may well be beneficial in the context of other diseases."[30] This conclusion echoes an earlier article in the same journal reviewing the relation between diet and heart disease:

> A generation of research on the diet-heart question has ended in disarray. The official line since 1950 for management of the epidemic of coronary heart disease has been a dietary treatment. Foundations, scientists and the media, both lay and scientific, have promoted low fat, low cholesterol polyunsaturated diets, and yet the epidemic continues unabated, cholesteremia in the population is unchanged and clinicians are unconvinced of efficacy. . . . One of the originators of the diet-heart hypothesis, E. H. Ahrens, Jr., wrote in 1969 and has restated in recent Congressional testimony, "It is not proven that dietary modification can prevent arteriosclerotic heart disease in man."[31]

The relation between disease and stress, a second component in the lifestyle hypothesis, is also questionable. The very nature of stress, in fact, is unclear; the concept tends to slip away from a direct gaze. The authors of *Healthy People* wrote, "When stress —or an individual's reaction to it—is excessive, physiological change can be so dramatic as to have serious physical and emotional consequences,"[32] thus leaving unanswered the question of whether stress is objective or subjective. Stress researchers disagree about whether stress causes the physiological change which has "physical and emotional consequences" or whether stress *is* the physical and emotional phenomena. Attempts to define the term more sharply characterize the introductory portions of most articles on stress. As chapter five shows, the widely differing results reveal the concept's elusive quality and raise questions about the suitability of stress as a topic for scientific research.[33]

As for exercise and physical fitness, they may prevent disease, and then again they may not. *Healthy People* admits they are only "attractive and plausible" as potential methods of disease prevention, while at the same time saying that "regular, vigorous exercise was found [in a study of Harvard alumni] to reduce risk of heart disease independent of other risk factors such as cigarette smoking or high blood pressure."[34] At the time *Healthy People* was written, scientists were still carrying on a protracted debate over the health effects of exercise. The controversy more or less ended with the 1979 report of coronary atherosclerosis in four marathon runners. Now all that most scientists are willing to say about the benefit of jogging is that it is good for the mind.[35]

It is perhaps not surprising that a number of scientists also question the role of smoking in disease causality. With the exception of tobacco industry scientists and their supporters, no one doubts that smoking is a major cause of both cancer and heart disease. Researchers do argue, however, about the extent of its importance. In a letter to *Science*, one critic points out that lung cancer rates among nonsmokers have doubled in the last twenty years, that lung cancer keeps increasing even though smoking has decreased over the last three decades, and that smoking does not account for the large geographic differences in lung cancer, whereas exposure to polluted occupational and ambient air does.[36]

While new data on the effects of passive smoking may help to explain this discrepancy, this particular critic joins many scientists in arguing that lung cancer is caused by several toxins working together. Certainly everyone agrees that smokers exposed to certain occupational and environmental pollutants (particularly asbestos) have a far greater chance of developing lung cancer than do people who do not smoke, and it is possible that most interpretations of the data overestimate the proportion of cancers attributable to smoking and underestimate that attributable to other factors.[37]

Political implications. Despite all these questions about the evidence supporting it, the lifestyle theory is the centerpiece of U.S. chronic disease prevention policy. There are three explanations for its popularity. First, many people champion it because the practices it requires have come to stand for individualism and upward mobility. In some circles, it is chic not to smoke, to jog around the streets, to exercise in gyms, to eat low-cholesterol foods. Doing these things, or claiming to do them ("We hardly ever eat meat any more"; "I've started running again"), testifies to membership in the affluent classes. Such behavior means you are economically successful, or expect to be, or at least are very much like people who are. It has come to demonstrate a willingness to work to improve yourself and an eagerness to move up socially. Moreover, whether or not all this activity prolongs life and wards off disease, it usually gives people a sense of well-being. Thus, like the personal behavior theory in the nineteenth century, the lifestyle theory stands for self-reliance and at the same time it makes you feel good.

The second reason for this theory's popularity is that it emphasizes personal control over disease. In an era where the news media continually publicize new threats to health from polluted water, air, and soil, and where both industrial disasters and the possibility of nuclear war pose threats completely outside the control of individual citizens, it is comforting to think that personal action can reduce one's chances of dying early. Whether lifestyle change calls for wearing a respirator at work, giving up cigarettes, or learning stress reduction techniques, it means that at least some disease is a consequence of circumstances over which individuals have control. In addition it suggests that health can be secured without major changes in industrial practices, in the economy, or in the government.[38] Thus it curiously echoes the latter-day miasma theory.

Policy makers themselves supply a third explanation for the theory's popularity: if the science supporting it is sound, lifestyle change may reduce medical care expenditures. Canada's 1974 report entitled *A New Perspective on the Health of Canadians*, which served U.S. policy makers as a model, was rooted in a desire to combat the high cost of doctors and hospitals.[39] In the United States the economic rationale for the lifestyle theory was expressed clearly in a 1979 editorial in *Science*: "Even though this is the richest nation in the world, the average American family . . . cannot afford to be ill. . . . President Carter and Senator Kennedy have both proposed national health insurance plans. . . . But as the debate over these multibillion-dollar plans heats up, the nation risks losing sight of the fact that one of the cheapest and most effective ways to put a cap on spiraling health care costs is through greater self-care."[40] So the theory is connected to fiscal prudence, just as the miasma theory once was. It is even better, because the prevention policies it implies cost the government virtually nothing. Changing one's lifestyle means participation in a societywide effort to reduce the amount of public money spent on medical care.

Given these powerful meanings, the lifestyle theory has withstood the objections of its opponents, even when the critics' central argument is that the prevention policies the theory engenders will not work. First, the critics say, the lifestyle theory does not address itself to the population most likely to become ill: the poor. It ignores the unequal abilities of people to change their habits, disregarding the differences between the laborer who punches a time clock—sometimes at two jobs—and who lives in the slums, and the executive with discretion over his or her working hours who lives in the suburbs. The lifestyle theory, they say, unfairly demands from these different kinds of people the same kinds of behavior. At bottom, the critics claim that behavior is a result of the conditions in which people live. They think that the lifestyle theory, by implying that people get sick because they are lazy and irresponsible, fails to recognize a causal connection between individual behavior and social norms and rewards. Howard Berliner remarks that talking about "lifestyle changes without first discussing the changes in the social conditions which give rise to them, without recognizing that lifestyle is derivative . . . is misleading."[41]

More pointedly, Leon Eisenberg argues that primary responsibility for health lies beyond the individual:

> The new converts to prevention, having discovered that behavior affects health, focus on the responsibility of the individual for illness prevention by eating and drinking in moderation, exercising properly, not smoking and the like. Surely, in the final analysis, it is the individual who carries out these actions. But what does it mean to hold the individual responsible for smoking when the government subsidizes tobacco farming, permits tax deductions for cigarette advertising and fails to use its taxing power as a disincentive to smoking? What does it mean to castigate the individual for poor eating habits when the public is inundated by advertisements for "empty-calorie" fast foods and is reinforced in present patterns of consumption by federal farm policy?[42]

These and other critics basically argue that both disease and lifestyle result from fundamental economic and political institutions. From this perspective, the emphasis on lifestyle as a cause of disease obscures the primary causes of poor health while at the same time, precisely by ignoring those causes, serves to strengthen an unjust status quo. Many critics of the lifestyle theory evidently agree with its prescriptions—especially the no-smoking component—so none actually proposes that standard health education programs be abolished. They do not argue that cigarette smoking is benign, nor that sedentary living or high-fat diets are healthy. Nor do they say that people have no responsibility for their health. What they object to is a disease prevention policy that puts the burden of change on individuals. Better health, they say, requires social change.

A second group of critics do not complain that the lifestyle theory misunderstands the causes of human behavior. They object to it because they find the environmental theory more compelling. These critics believe that chemicals, radiation, and other toxins are at least equally responsible for chronic diseases, and they think that an emphasis on personal lifestyle as a cause of disease makes the public less likely to place a high priority on cleaning up the environment.[43]

ENVIRONMENTAL THEORY

The environmental theory even more significantly challenges the chain of causality implied by the germ theory. It holds that significant numbers of chronic diseases are caused by toxins in the environment, and it implies that disease prevention, instead of requiring personal change or medical treatments, demands changes in industrial production. Three government agencies are based on the environmental hypothesis, each addressing different kinds of hazards. The Occupational Health and Safety Administration (OSHA) regulates hazards in the workplace; the Environmental Protection Agency (EPA) regulates hazards in the ambient environment; and the Food and Drug Administration regulates hazards in food.

The first aspect of the environmental hypothesis is occupational hazards. The best known and possibly the most serious example is asbestos, some six hundred thousand tons of which are still used annually in the United States.[44] An estimated 27.5 million men and women were potentially exposed to asbestos from 1940 through 1979.[45] The government has estimated that 58,000–78,000 of these men and women will die excess deaths each year: the largest number from lung cancer, a smaller number from abdominal and chest malignancies, and still others from asbestosis, a respiratory disease caused by scarring of the lungs.[46] But asbestosis is by no means the only occupational hazard.

An ever-growing list of chemical compounds has been linked to diseases among workers in dozens of occupations. In the words of the Department of Health and Human Services (DHHS), "Toxic effects have been reported for nearly 45,000 to 50,000 chemicals which are thought to appear in the workplace —over 2,000 of which are suspected human carcinogens in laboratory animals."[47] In addition to cancer, some occupational toxins are implicated in heart disease, for toxins that cause respiratory illnesses (the main occupational disease) can also exacerbate heart disease. Years of pumping blood through inelastic lung tissues puts a severe strain on the heart. Heart disease, in fact, is number five in the government's list of the ten most common occupational diseases and injuries.[48]

Workers in hazardous environments include uranium workers, coalminers, people exposed to cotton dust, agricultural workers, welders, coke oven attendants, barbers and hairdressers, carpenters, textile printers, drug makers, dry cleaners, rubber workers, electrical workers, oil processors, and metalworkers. In sum, the majority of blue-collar workers and many white-collar workers as well spend many hours each day in environments where chemical fumes, dusts, mists, and vapors may endanger their health.

Precisely how much danger workers face is simply not known, a situation some scientists—and workers—interpret as critical while others find it relatively undisturbing. Among the concerned are the members of a study group convened in 1984 by the National Research Council to look at chemical toxicity information. These scientists reported that between 80 and 90 percent of the chemicals used in commerce, drug manufacture, pesticides, cosmetics, and food have never been tested for health hazards. Acknowledging that the majority of chemicals do not need testing because they are unlikely to be dangerous, the report said that nevertheless the chemicals that should be tested for health effects number in the tens of thousands.[49]

What distinguishes the environmental theory from the germ and lifestyle theories is not so much the lack of information (scientists also have inadequate knowledge about viruses, diet, exercise, stress, and tobacco) as that the sources of possible harm keep expanding. Estimates of the number of new chemicals with unknown health effects introduced yearly into industry go as high as one thousand.[50] In addition, the growing sophistication in laboratory technology means that diseases can be linked to smaller and smaller amounts of a chemical so that substances once thought safe are sometimes now considered dangerous. The presumed remedy for this situation, the Toxic Substances Control Act of 1976, has proven almost useless. Designed to control chemicals before they are introduced into the environment, it is inadequately funded and riddled with loopholes.

Although workers, because of the high concentrations and heavy exposures in the workplace, run the most serious risks from unknown substances that are poorly controlled, the health of the general public may also be affected. Thus the second aspect of the environmental hypothesis concentrates on toxic substances in the air, water, and soil. The presence of organic chemical carcinogens in drinking water supplies has been known for decades, but today drinking water is far more contaminated than it was a generation ago.[51] According to the Office of Technology Assessment, some 175 organic chemicals occur in groundwater, the source of drinking water for 50 percent of the nation's population and 80 percent of rural residents. Many of these chemicals are known or suspected carcinogens, and others cause such health effects as central nervous system damage, liver and kidney disease, and eye and skin irritation.[52] Environmental theorists fear that the numbers and amounts of chemicals in all drinking water sources will grow as the chemical industry grows—and as companies search for ways to comply with laws intended to control chemical wastes in other media.

Besides water pollution, waste treatment efforts may also have increased air pollution. The only national survey of toxic chemicals in the air, undertaken by a congressional subcommittee in 1985, found that industries spew more than sixty-two million pounds of toxic chemicals into the air, far more than formerly thought. At least 120 different chemicals are involved, and most of them are unregulated for health effects.[53] The Clean Air Act offers little assurance that it will address this situation. Established primarily to curb smog, the act pays scant attention to cancer agents. Under it, the EPA has set national standards for only fourteen substances. Seven are relatively benign air contaminants (called "criteria pollutants"), and on these the EPA has always concentrated regulatory action. The seven others are carcinogens (called "hazardous substances") but these are regulated not in the ambient air but only as emissions from certain categories of industries. All other air pollution regulations come from the states—a situation that has produced a patchwork of conflicting standards—and little data exist to show that the standards protect against disease. On the contrary, epidemiologic surveys have found significantly increased lung cancer mortality rates in communities near paper, chemical, petroleum, and transportation industries.[54]

In addition to industrial wastes, the air and water can be contaminated by pesticides. According to the EPA, pesticides contain approximately fifteen hundred active ingredients, one-third of which are toxic and one-fourth carcinogenic.[55] These pesticides are often highly volatile, escaping into the air and water in agricultural communities and sometimes leaving residues in the soil for years after application. They accumulate in the food chain and can be recovered later in dairy products, meat, poultry, and fish.

Advocates of the environmental theory of disease causality place particular stress on radioactivity. The EPA estimates that by the year 2000, commercial nuclear reactors will have generated one hundred thousand metric tons of high-level radioactive wastes and one billion cubic feet of low-level wastes.[56] It is not at all clear that plans for storing and disposing of these wastes are adequate. Low-level radiation, increasingly reported as presenting a greater risk than previously suspected, endangers not only nuclear plant workers but people who receive even routine x rays.[57] Until very recently only cancer had been linked to radiation, but a new study for the National Institute of Occupational Safety and Health suggests that cardiovascular disease and stroke may also be consequences.[58]

Toxic waste dumps, a recent but now central focus of the environmental theory, in many ways epitomize the issue. As new laws force industries to control toxins they once released into the air and water, the number of dump sites grows. Today between 250 and 270 million metric tons of hazardous waste are produced each year in the United States, 90 percent of which is improperly disposed of.[59] The EPA estimates that more than thirty thousand abandoned or inactive hazardous waste dumps exist in the United States. No one knows exactly what chemicals any of these dumps contain or precisely how they effect human health.[60] "A major toxicological problem," says the DHHS, "is that humans are likely to be exposed to combinations or mixtures of chemicals. There are virtually no data on or experience in testing mixtures of chemicals for potential health effects."[61]

A third aspect of the environmental theory concerns synthetic additives to foods. The U.S. House Committee on Interstate and Foreign Commerce reports that "virtually all food contains residues of synthetic substances that have been developed in recent decades. Scores of these chemicals have been linked to cancer, birth defects and permanent genetic mutations. Still others have never been tested for safety."[62] American grocery shoppers purchase along with their food some three thousand direct additives (i.e., preservatives, flavorings, stabilizers, and colors) and ten thousand indirect additives (chemicals connected with processing, packing, and storing) plus an unknown number of additional environmental contaminants.[63]

The DHHS presented a succinct précis of the environmental theory of disease causality to Congress in 1980: "In summary, we believe that toxic chemicals are adding to the disease burden of the United States in a significant although as yet not precisely defined way."[64]

Disputes. Two scientific disputes surround the environmental hypothesis. The first concerns the suitability of extrapolating from animals to human beings. Most of the data on which environmental standards are based comes from toxicology, in other words, from laboratory studies with animals. In the typical study, scientists administer the substance in question to rats and then study their response compared with a group of controls. But they give rats doses many times greater than humans would be expected to receive. The reason is that most rats, like humans, show no response to the substance, so enormously large numbers of rats would be necessary to detect a toxin administered at doses corresponding to human exposure. Samuel Epstein explains the rationale:

> Let us suppose that humans and rats are equally sensitive to some chemical carcinogen which causes one case of cancer in every 10,000 persons (or rats) to which it is given. If 22,000,000 Americans were exposed to this chemical, 22,000 cases of cancer would occur. On the other hand, if fed to the typical fifty rats used in an experiment, the chances that even one rat would get cancer is one-half of one percent; 10,000 rats would have to be fed the chemical (at human dosages) to observe even one cancer.
>
> Given that a human-level dosage might not produce a detectable result in a small rat population . . . the only alternative is to increase the dose, and thereby increase the probability of inducing cancer in a particular animal.[65]

Such experiments teach scientists a lot about the toxicity of the chemical in one strain of rats subjected to high doses. The question is—and this is the heart of the debate among scientists— what happens to human beings? People come in many strains and physical conditions and are usually exposed to low doses. How can you extrapolate from animals to humans?

Some scientists argue that you cannot. Gio Batta Gori, for

example, as deputy director of the National Cancer Institute, pointed out that animal tests bias the results in favor of finding carcinogens because research protocol calls for using the most sensitive species and administering the suspected carcinogen in the way most likely to cause cancer. Listing a variety of reasons for uncertainty in animal tests he said, "Discouraging as it may seem, it is not plausible that animal carcinogenesis experiments can be improved to the point where quantitative generalizations about human risks can be drawn from them."[66]

Other scientists disagree. Richard R. Bates, of the National Institutes of Environmental Health Services, writes that it is appropriate to

> rely on experimental studies with animals as a base for judging the potential carcinogenicity of a chemical for human beings. The practice is supported by the observation that most known human carcinogens are also carcinogenic in experimental animals, that for the most part the same kind of metabolic enzymes that activate and detoxify chemical carcinogens are present in both human and animal tissues and in experimental animals and that the general process of development of similar kinds of cancer is comparable in human and experimental animals.[67]

The second dispute revolves around the concept of threshold levels. It may or may not be possible to determine levels of exposure to a carcinogen below which people are not in danger of getting cancer. By setting precise permissible exposure levels for carcinogens, OSHA and the EPA implicitly affirm that threshold levels can be determined. Both agencies have also asserted, however, that there is no mechanism for determining the existence of thresholds for chemical carcinogens and, therefore, that any dose should be considered carcinogenic.[68]

The American Industrial Hygiene Council, an industry group, takes the opposite view. When he chaired the council's scientific committee, Dr. Fred Hoerger of Dow Chemical claimed "no-effect levels have been repeatedly demonstrated for carcinogens in animals and man."[69] Similarly, Gori says that the presence of thresholds is "suggested by much evidence which parallels universally accepted concepts in chemistry, physiology and pharmacology."[70]

Bates, of the National Institutes of Environmental Health Services, suggests that some of the controversy over thresholds results from a confusion over whether the term is applied to populations or individuals, but he concludes that "we are still in a position of being unable to unequivocally decide whether or not thresholds exist, as defined at the molecular or population level."[71]

Political implications. These medical issues would not engage us, nor would they elicit such passion from scientists, were it not for the political issues underlying them. The environmental hypothesis, as I have described it, points to industrial production as the cause of disease and forces its proponents to the conclusion that to have a healthy population we must make changes in the economy. In other words, it wears its politics on its sleeve, in marked contrast to the germ theory and the lifestyle theory, which, although as "political" as the environmental theory, appear to be neutral because they do not challenge the status quo. The extent to which the environmental theory of disease causality challenges current arrangements depends, however, on what is meant by the term *environment*.

In the 1970s proponents of the environmental theory gave wide publicity to John Higgenson's estimate that 80–90 percent of all cancers are environmental. Higgenson, founder of the World Health Organization's prestigious International Agency for Research on Cancer, now says that he has been misunderstood. By "environmental" he meant lifestyle factors. In a 1979 interview in *Science*, he denied the interpretation that toxins in the air and water play a major role in cancer. "From an epidemiological viewpoint," he said, "I believe that attempts to prevent most tumors through control only of mutagens and carcinogens will prove to be a disappointing approach." He went on to assert that smoking, diet, and "behavior" are the most important causes of cancer. An "overemphasis on chemical carcinogens has distorted our approach," he said. "To make cancer the whipping boy for every environmental evil may prevent effective action when it does matter, as with cigarettes."[72]

He got the metaphor twisted, but obviously Higgenson meant that blaming the environment for cancer is ineffective, partly because the environment does not cause much cancer, but also because people can do little to change the environment. In contrast, he implied, people can do much to change personal behavior. Whether or not the environment is more or less easily changed than behavior, Higgenson's distinction illuminates the reasons for an argument about the definition of "the environment." If the concept refers to the air, water, and soil, then the major responsibility for disease rests with those who pollute. If the concept refers mostly to smoking, eating, and other forms of behavior, then the responsibility for disease is largely personal. This second interpretation implies that there is no real environmental cause of disease distinguishable from a behavioral cause, and thus little need for a prevention policy focused on industry.

Even among people who believe that environmental carcinogens are a significant source of disease, there is disagreement about what the word *environment* means. For most toxicologists and epidemiologists, it is a general term for the place where disease-causing chemicals, fibers, and radiation are found, just as it is a place where disease-causing microorganisms are found. To the extent that this definition prevails, the environmental theory of disease causality is no different from the germ theory. It presents unique methodological difficulties, but just as in the germ theory, scientists can focus on the toxins themselves and the effects they have on the body. For them, it is not so much that the environment causes disease as it is that certain environmental *substances* cause disease.

Other people, however, think that "the environment" refers to a whole and that environmental diseases cannot be effectively controlled if the term is conceptually reduced to its constituents. From this perspective, the environment, instead of being simply that place where the cause of disease is found, becomes the cause itself. To see the difference between these two positions, consider a group of workers exposed to a toxin like benzidine that puts them at increased risk for bladder cancer. If "the environment" is merely the passive element which contains benzidine, disease prevention appropriately concentrates on the chemical, not the air in which it is found. The exposed workers would be urged, or required, to wear respirators on the job. If "the environment" is more ubiquitous—the air itself, say, or the workplace in general—disease prevention is less likely to concentrate on placing barriers between the worker and the toxin (a tactic that leaves the toxin in the air), and more likely to concentrate on cleaning the air. One method puts responsibility on the workers, much like the lifestyle theory; the other puts responsibility on the owners and managers of industry.

Which sort of chronic disease prevention policy prevails depends largely on how the term *environment* comes to be understood. Many powerful groups of people have an interest—however unconscious—in making it mean something compatible with either the lifestyle or the germ theory of disease causality. If their views come to predominate, the environmental theory will not likely usher in a second public health revolution. It will collapse into an individualistic view of disease causality, supporting both the germ theory's excessively technical approach to prevention and the lifestyle theory's ignorance of the social sources of behavior. Should this happen, the likelihood that the government will develop really effective chronic disease prevention policies is slim.

CHAPTER 3

A Multicausal
Solution?

No doubt some readers have gone through the previous two chapters impatiently. Who cares what political meanings the various theories acquire or how they attribute responsibility? To these readers, distinctions among theories of disease causality are academic exercises. They probably say that no one really believes in discrete causes for disease any more. Both chronic and infectious diseases are clearly multicausal. Only the naive would advance a simple germ or behavioral or environmental theory of disease causality. Epidemiology, these critics might point out, has long since discarded the linear model in which disease is caused primarily by biology, secondarily by behavior, and finally by broadly defined environmental factors. It has for many years even enlarged and elaborated on the host-agent-environment triad wherein each of these factors affects the other. The new, multicausal model shows that a huge number of phenomena go together to produce illnesses: agents that contaminate the air, water, soil, or food; psychological stress; lack of access to preventive medicine; unhealthy personal behavior; certain political and economic institutions; and genetic predisposition. In addition, many of these phenomena give rise to and result from intangibles like political ideology, economic power, and social obligations.

Indeed, such readers have a point. Authors of the newer epidemiology textbooks commonly advance the concept that disease is multifactorial. Distinguishing this idea from older, less complex views of disease causality, they emphasize the intricate reciprocal interactions among disease-causing events. It is evident, say Brian MacMahon and Thomas Pugh, "that the chains of causation represent only a fraction of the reality, and the whole genealogy may be thought of more appropriately as a web, which in its complexity and origins lies quite beyond our understanding."[1] Similarly, Mervyn Susser says that since "agent and host are engaged in continuing interaction with an enveloping environment . . . the interrelationships are appropriately described in terms like 'web,' 'network,' or 'configuration.'"[2]

In some ways these analogies are felicitous and useful. Causality is complex. A web model, more effectively than a linear or triadic configuration, represents the reality that disease occurs in a social, physical, political, psychological, cultural, and economic *context.* Webs indicate that a rich variety of causes contribute to disease and that these causes are redundant and self-reinforcing. Webs warn us of the simple-mindedness of considering diseases as elementary occurrences.[3] They also help to depict causality on many levels, for each of the factors listed above is composed of subfactors. Unhealthy behavior, for example, is linked to poor education, bad role models, sloth, commercial advertising, and so on. Exposure to environmental toxins results from weak laws, scientific debate, human error, refusal to use protective equipment, economic necessity, and more. The process of carcinogenesis itself is most accurately described as multicausal. For instance, arsenic alone does not produce cancer; it apparently interacts with the immune response, dietary deficiencies, and trace metal imbalances.[4] Similarly, leukemia seems to require several events—viruses, bacteria, chemicals, and mechanical insults—all operating in synergy.

Webs also appeal because they promise to redress the fragmented physical and social sciences. The concept forces academics out of their narrow disciplines, encouraging them to produce a richer, more accurate picture of reality. In their perceptive book on American ideology, Robert Bellah and his colleagues recognize "a sense of fragmentariness" in both intellectual and popular cultures. "Starting with science," they say, "the most respected and influential part of our high culture, we can see at once that it is not a whole, offering a general interpretation of reality, as theology and philosophy once did, but a collection of disciplines each having little to do with the others."[5] To Bellah and the others, the popularity in universities of "core courses" derives from a recognition that the regular cafeteria-style curriculum, serving up knowledge in discrete portions, presents an incoherent picture of the world. They call instead for a "social ecology" that treats humans and society as deeply interrelated: "It is only in the context of society as a whole, with its possibilities, its limitations, and its aspirations, that particular variables can be understood."[6]

To see "variables" in their social context is to question the very logic underpinning scientific methodology. And indeed the multicausal idea fits neatly into the contemporary challenge to positivism. Like hermeneutics, ethnomethodology, and structuralism, it takes a stand against reductionist Cartesian dualism. It is consistent with the postmodernist proposition that reality is a viewpoint filtered through the subjectivity of the viewer. The concept is not even new. John Stuart Mill, writing over a century ago on the identification of cause, asserted, "The real Cause, is the whole of these antecedents; and we have, philosophically speaking, no right to give the name of cause to one of them exclusive of the others. . . . All the conditions are equally indispensable to the production of the consequent; and the statement of the cause is incomplete, unless in some shape or other we introduce them all."[7]

Regardless of its superiority over the old linear and triad views, however, the multifactorial model of disease causality may be as incapable of directing a truly effective disease prevention policy as the theories it replaces. Ironically, its weakness lies in its very attempt to present all causes of disease. Moreover, its effect is to reinforce the status quo. Because the multicausal theory of disease is so highly acclaimed, it is the focus of this chapter. Instead of following the format of the previous chapters and examining the social contexts from which causal theories emerge, this chapter takes a more forthrightly critical tack. It describes the drawbacks of the multifactorial theory, looks at an alternative explanation, and discusses the criteria for an efficacious concept of disease causality.

One hears most about the multicausal theory as an explanation for chronic illnesses. Indeed, some of policy makers' helplessness in the face of cardiovascular disease and cancer comes from assuming an inherent difference between chronic and infectious diseases. But the common impression that microorganisms cause infectious disease whereas many factors cause heart disease and cancer is wrong.[8] Infectious diseases can validly be depicted as multicausal. To say that infectious diseases are monocausal confuses the *agent* of disease with the *cause* of disease. The agent of an infectious disease—a bacteria, virus, or parasite—may be necessary, but it is never sufficient.[9] As Milton Terris puts it:

> There are no single causes of infectious diseases; their causes are multiple and entwined in a web of causation which is often more complex than that of many noninfectious diseases. It is well known that the causes of cholera in India today go back hundreds of years in India's history, to the British invasion and destruction of once-flourishing textile industries; the maintenance of archaic systems of land ownership and tillage; the persistence of the caste system and the unbelievable poverty, hunger, and crowding; the consequent inability to afford the development of safe water supplies and sewage disposal systems; and, almost incidently, the presence of cholera vibrios.[10]

Moreover, others have even questioned the idea that diseases have *necessary* agents. MacMahon and Pugh point to the concept's circular reasoning: a disease is defined as that biologic state produced by the organism in question. Furthermore, "the distinction between necessary causes—those without which the disease does not occur—and contributory causes" is arbitrary. For example, MacMahon and Pugh continue, although the tubercle bacillus is usually called the necessary cause of tuberculosis—and nutritional status one of the contributing causes—

"had medical knowledge developed differently [the bacillus] might have been included in the definition of a specific nutritional defect. In that case, the nutritional defect would have been the necessary cause and the bacillus a contributory factor."[11] So it is as inappropriate to label infectious disease monocausal as it is to call chronic disease monocausal. But to say that these diseases are multicausal has several drawbacks.

SHORTCOMINGS

First, the concept gives few clues about how to prevent disease. As MacMahon and Pugh put it, the "complexity and origins [of causality] lie quite beyond our understanding."[12] The clear guidelines for action implicit in the germ theory's linear model here all subdivide, point to yet other causal factors, double back on one another, go both ways at once, and never lead *out* anywhere. The multifactorial model would be a maze except that there are no dead ends: everything is linked to everything else.[13] Worse, the intricate connecting links make any one preventive action appear insignificant. To be effective, prevention policy seemingly has to attack all possible causes at once—a strategy that would stretch available resources far beyond their capacity and end up by devoting only a pittance to each. In practice, the multicausal model easily becomes a rationale for not taking action. Since everything is connected to everything, we are apparently hopelessly knotted into our own cultural practices, products, and institutions. Thus we either have to accept the diseases that evidently go along with them or opt for revolution. Some tinkering around the edges is possible, but by and large, the multifactorial web seems to show, real disease prevention is nearly impossible. Better to concentrate on cure. It may be more expensive, but it is simpler.

In this respect, the epidemiologist's multicausal web is close cousin to structural functionalism, the sociological theory principally associated with Talcott Parsons.[14] Parsons developed a view of the world that has been widely—and frequently unconsciously—adopted by social scientists. By this view, humans live in "social systems" composed of interdependent parts all functioning together in equilibrium, much like the human body. Structural functionalism was central to social analysis for a whole generation of social scientists but has been under increasing attack for its misrepresentation of reality and its conservative bias. The critics point out that it ignores the histories of societies, thus making them appear natural; it avoids the recognition of conflict, thus offering no explanation for change; and it makes change in any one part of the interrelated elements seem to threaten the whole, thus cautioning against political activism.[15]

There is a second drawback to the multicausal view. When policy makers do propose disease prevention programs, the web model permits them to mislead the public about the efficacy of their proposals. Because the model assigns equal importance to each aspect of causality, it treats all hypotheses about disease causality as though they were essentially alike, merely different facets of a large "multifactorial" cause.[16] This generous egalitarianism makes it easy to direct disease prevention resources to ineffective but socially nondisruptive programs—instead of to effective but disruptive ones—*without* public discussion of these options. It allows the DHHS, to take an influential example, to warn about environmental pollutants as a cause of disease but to advocate primarily lifestyle changes as the means of prevention. The DHHS publication *Healthy People* is paradigmatic of this practice.[17] The Occupational Safety and Health Administration uses a similar strategy. In most states, its worker education program is heavily oriented toward individual responsibility for disease prevention, even though the agency itself was predicated on the theory that industry is responsible. Hence OSHA personnel tend to preach behavior change—wearing respirators, special clothing, earplugs, safety glasses—as the main means of preventing occupational disease and to downplay the strategy of changing plant design.[18]

Malnutrition, most dramatically in the Third World, provides another example. The multicausal model includes explanations on all levels. A frequently cited Rockefeller Foundation book on health in the Third World mentions the following causes: nonavailability of food, poverty, unhealthy eating patterns, traditional community structure, crowding, ignorance, poor ventilation, filth and flies, lack of good medical care, and overpopulation.[19] Most other texts also set down these causes, although many refer in addition to agricultural practices, and most also note the presence of infectious and parasitic diseases.[20] Well-meaning but politically cautious heads of relief organizations can pick and choose freely among the "balanced" list of causes, a task made easy because the list includes causes on different levels of abstraction. Since all of these phenomena together cause malnutrition, the list offers no inherent reason to choose "poverty" over "unavailability of food" regardless of the fact that the former is a fundamental cause whereas the latter is secondary. When aid agencies operate as though lack of food were the basic problem, their efforts (e.g., food supplements, the Green Revolution) clearly do save the lives of some people. But the social structure that perpetuates malnutrition among a large percentage of the population, year after year, generation after generation, remains untouched.[21]

This equal weighting of causes also means that those who have something to lose from prevention programs can insist that the factor for which they have no responsibility is the real cause. For example, asbestos companies can insist that smoking is the real cause of lung disease, and cigarette companies can insist that occupational exposure is the culprit. Smokers themselves can take their pick. The multicausal web by itself offers no clear challenge to these positions.

The third drawback to the multicausal theory is that the actual prevention policies it implies would be inefficient in many cases. To illustrate, imagine its implementation were we to learn tomorrow that the cholera organism contaminates our water supply. In such an emergency the multicausal view would direct us to divide disease prevention resources among at least three programs: one to inoculate the population against cholera, another to administer a health education campaign to teach people the best way to boil water (and how to prepare food, bathe, brush their teeth, and swim without ingesting any), and a third to pu-rify water of the cholera bacterium. But of course, such a policy would be highly unpopular, and rightly so. Rather than preven-tive medicine and health education, most Americans would ex-pect first priority to go to ensuring that they got pure water when they turned on the tap. (Then, naturally, there would be no need for health education programs or mass inoculations.) If this ensurance required changes for some local business or in-dustry, some challenge to political or economic privilege, the public's health would seem to supersede these interests. Even in the case of yellow fever—a disease unlike cholera in that a truly effective vaccine exists—we would want a mosquito-eradication program aimed at the physical and political environment, not a health education program aimed at the people or a vaccination program aimed at the microorganism. In the continued pres-ence of infected mosquitoes, the latter two programs require for their success nearly perfect compliance by virtually the entire population, on and on forever. Thus no matter how well imple-mented, they have a higher likelihood of failure than does a vigorous effort to eradicate *Aedes aegypti*. The same reasoning should hold for chronic diseases. The fact that it frequently does not—that the public is often willing to accept weak chronic dis-ease prevention efforts—is a topic I take up in chapter seven. (To anticipate that discussion, such willingness attests to the power of an individualistic ideology.)

I do not wish to imply that disease prevention should never address the agent of disease. Despite the fact that "having" the agent does not necessarily mean becoming ill,[22] and despite the fact that concentration on the agent can depoliticize disease, thus making control harder in the long run,[23] and despite the fact that effective disease prevention can occur without knowl-edge of the agent,[24] attention to the agent, if there is one, usu-ally enhances disease prevention programs. Consider deaths from gunshot. The anti–gun control lobby argues that guns do not kill people, people kill people. Surely, that is logical; re-duction of violent deaths depends on a great deal more than banning or registering firearms. Nevertheless, controlling the private possession of guns is an important step toward lessening those deaths. In the same vein, war is not caused by the presence of bombs; instead bombs exist because of hostilities among nations. But reducing weaponry at least diminishes the possibility that international hostilities will result in war.[25] And the actual elimination of smallpox worldwide uncorrelated with political and economic change shows that for at least one disease, concentration on the agent was enough. In most cases, however, to be effective, an attack on the agent must be secondary to an attack on the fundamental cause.

A fourth shortcoming of the multicausal theory is the gap between what it promises and what epidemiologists deliver. Terris complains that even with the model of a multicausal web in their minds, most epidemiologists spend their time searching for identifiable risk factors, precisely as though they were looking for particular disease agents. In the end, they ignore the complex of social factors the web depicts, apparently considering the term *multiple causation* a cloak for inadequate knowledge.[26]

Technology itself is partly responsible for this incongruity between the idea of a multicausal web and the practices of epidemiologists. The tools available to them limit what they can study. They can say that psychological disposition or social obligations or economic power contribute to disease, but their actual analyses can only employ empirical phenomena. They necessarily leave out exactly those nonquantifiable phenomena that constitute the strength of the web idea. It is possible to calculate the separate effects of various factors and even the interactive effects of some (smoking and asbestos, for example) but that is not enough. The web says that disease is caused by the interaction of all the factors. The model represents the idea that the total cause is greater than the sum of its parts. The whole *pattern* is at issue, including the nebulous, abstract relationships created among the separate factors. Take political power for example. It constitutes an important strand in the web of disease causality, but it cannot be discovered or located empirically in any one factor. Political power is a relationship, not a thing. It is part of the web of causality, but precisely because it is a relationship, it cannot be part of a strictly scientific study of the web. Hans Enzensberger, writing about the new interest in ecology, makes a similar point: "The mediation between the whole and the part, between subsystem and global system, cannot be explained by the tools of biology. This mediation is social, and its explication requires an elaborated social theory and at the very least some basic assumptions about the historical process. Neither the one nor the other is available to present-day ecologists."[27]

So the textbooks that begin with the observation that a multitude of empirical and nonempirical phenomena interact to produce disease, progress to examples that reduce the causes to phenomena expressable in numbers. Common among them are age, sex, geographic location, socioeconomic status, diet, years of education, race, cigarette consumption, exposure to disease agents, and so on. Despite the sheer quantity of these factors (and advancements in computer technology allow epidemiologists to add ever more factors to the analysis), they are necessarily only phenomena of one sort: empirical, discrete, and meaningless in themselves. The methodology has served admirably to reveal hitherto hidden, specific relationships—between radiation and leukemia, for example, or tobacco and heart disease. But as a way to understand how myriad social, economic, political, psychological, historical, and aesthetic aspects of human life interact to produce disease, the methodology falls short. The multicausal web turns out to be a provocative idea but an impossible basis for statistical epidemiology. It is what Jackob Najman calls "another monocausal view applied to a number of different conditions."[28]

SCIENCE AND MULTICAUSALITY

The foregoing section criticizes the multicausal theory from a policy analyst's viewpoint. The classic scientific view, ironically, sees merit where policy analysis sees muddle. The inapplicability —the guidelessness, if you will—of the multicausal theory is exactly what is right with it. Its refusal to identify a single cause constitutes its strength. The web has an appeal for scientists because it appears to offer both a complete picture of disease causality and a means of remaining neutral on the question of policy. The scientist's task, as most scientists see it, is simply to present all the facts and leave to the policy makers the question of what action to take.

This position seems at first reasonable. As chapters one and two point out, causal models are always value laden when they pinpoint some one factor as the primary cause of disease. By implicitly placing responsibility on one sector of the population rather than another, they indicate where change will have to occur if the major diseases are to be controlled. Therefore science, to maintain neutrality, should avoid models that assign responsibility. Identifying all causes for an event would be an excellent way to steer clear of implicit policy statements.

Unfortunately, it would also be impossible. The list of causes, including all the physical, psychological, social, political, and economic elements, would extend back to the beginning of time and across virtually all aspects of life. As Max Weber put it, "An exhaustive causal investigation of any concrete phenomena in its full reality is not only impossible, it is simply nonsense."[29] Epidemiologists know this and do not attempt to include all causal factors in their analyses. They select some causes and omit others. Since the epidemiologist must, however, employ some criteria in the selection process, whether consciously or not, the final roundup of causes is never neutral. It necessarily reflects both the (human-made) rules of epidemiology and the values and assumptions of the person selecting the cause. The list probably reproduces many elements of the dominant political ideology as well, if only because the language we use to describe reality is so heavily influenced by the interests of powerful groups. For example, consider the case of smoking.

Everyone "knows" that cigarette smoking causes lung cancer. Accordingly, lung cancer prevention depends on getting people to stop smoking, and the multifactorial explanation for the disease emphasizes all the possible reasons for smoking. But suppose what we "knew" was that *tobacco* causes lung cancer. The term would not be just another way of saying the same thing. Naming tobacco instead of smoking as the cause would have several important consequences: causal analysis would more likely emphasize reasons for the presence of tobacco in the environment than reasons for the habit of smoking; lung cancer would be considered primarily an environmental disease with some behavioral aspects (rather than the other way around); and the promotion of smokeless tobacco would be exposed at the outset for the subversion that it is.

The scientific perspective offers another seductive but deceptive rationale for a multicausal approach: it is too risky to put all the eggs in one basket when science is unsure. According to this view, policy makers should practice caution in the face of scientific debate about the causes of disease. This appeal rests on the assumption that, in the absence of debate, scientific facts are both recognized and transformed into action. Perhaps proponents of the view have in mind the isolation of the polio virus and consequent development of immunization programs. They forget that numerous fatal diseases—not only polio but yellow fever, plague, cholera, dengue, and typhus—are still endemic in most of the Third World today, although the microscopic agents of these diseases have long been known to science. Perhaps, too, they do not realize that the much-acclaimed worldwide eradication of smallpox in the 1970s occurred more than one hundred-and-fifty years after the introduction of vaccination.[30] And perhaps they have not heard that the toxicity of asbestos, apparently a very recent discovery, had been so well established by 1918 that some U.S. and Canadian life insurance firms refused to sell policies to asbestos workers.[31] In other words, uncertainty about the cause of disease is seldom the reason for its prevalence. Even when the facts are undisputed, prevention can falter. More to the point, science is rarely sure. To call for absolute certainty and agreement among scientists before taking preventive action is merely a delaying tactic, effective only to the extent that people believe the myth that certainty characterizes science.

But more significantly, the appeal to caution evades a central political question: for whom is it too risky to put all the eggs in one basket? "If there is room for scientists to debate," demands Molly Coye, "why are workers exposed in the interim?" Answering her own question, she continues, "They are endangered not because of lack of conclusive information but because of *political assumptions about who takes the risk.* The notion of 'scientific neutrality' accepts these assumptions, implicitly siding with corporate industrial interests to postpone the protection of worker health."[32] The same point could be made about the population in general. While scientists debate, we ask that all people take the risk of living in an environment that may make them ill, instead of asking that owners of businesses and industries take the risk of losing money. To the extent that a multicausal model of disease restrains preventive action, it supports the status quo. When the status quo includes the presence of suspected toxins in the occupational and ambient environment, the lack of action is not neutral. It risks people's health.

An Alternative

I have argued against the multifactorial view of disease causality because it is a poor guide to effective prevention. It does not discriminate between fundamental and superficial causes of disease, so it allows policy makers to emphasize the more politically benign causes and to promote relatively inefficient prevention programs without having to justify these choices. Further, although the multifactorial web includes the causal roles played by political and economic power in disease causality, these roles are only weakly captured by the empirical methodology employed by most of the epidemiologists who champion it. Moreover, the multicausal view of disease hides its politics. Posing as a scientific theory of causality, and thus by definition as a politically neutral one, the multicausal theory and its application are nevertheless as influenced by values and beliefs as the monocausal theories it supplants.

Could some other theory of disease causality overcome these

drawbacks? Is there a way to envision disease that is neither a multicausal web nor a monocausal beeline? Such a theory would have to display a hierarchy of causality without being reductionistic, lend itself to effective prevention programs, and make room for nonempirical causes of disease. To find such a theory, we can first look at the early nineteenth century. At the time when the germ theory, the miasma theory, the supernatural theory, and the personal behavior theory contended for predominance, a handful of social critics began to develop a new perspective on disease causality: they said its origins were social. Among the early spokesmen for this point of view were Louis René Villermé and Pierre Cabanis in France, and Rudolf Leubuscher, Solomon Neumann, and Max von Pettenkofer in Germany.[33] But the most enduring descriptions of the social etiology of disease were written by Rudolf Virchow and Friedrich Engels.

Virchow was a brilliant pathologist, who is known today as the father of cellular biology.[34] Born in 1821, he published hundreds of scholarly papers during his long lifetime, was revered by his contemporaries, and analyzed the nature of medicine and science in such original and constructive ways that he is still quoted by the twentieth century's more philosophically minded scientists. In 1848 Virchow was sent from the hospital in Berlin where he was a junior lecturer in pathology to investigate a severe typhus epidemic and famine in Upper Silesia. Already active in the revolutionary political movements of the midcentury, already acutely aware of the poverty and injustice the revolutions hoped to address, Virchow saw direct linkages between the epidemic and the conditions under which poor people lived. He spent three weeks in Upper Silesia, and instead of producing the routine report such investigations usually elicit, he wrote a moving and detailed account of the social causes of disease.[35] In the final pages of his report, he proposed far-reaching political reforms as the only adequate means of avoiding future disasters. The way, he said, "to prevent outbreaks in Upper Silesia is quite simple: education, together with its daughters, freedom, and welfare." Elaborating, he specifically addressed the need for better roads, improved agriculture, regional and local self-government, and separation of church and state. "We have often referred to 'the scientific method,'" he said; "we now find that through applying it, we have moved from medicine into the social field, and in so doing, we have had to consider some of the fundamental issues of our times":[36]

> Mass education through primary, commercial and agricultural schools, cheap books and mass newspapers, combined with complete freedom of community life are the first demands which have to be granted to these people. . . . I insist that free and unlimited democracy is the single most important principle. If we get free and well-educated people then we shall undoubtedly have healthy ones as well. . . . A sound constitution must affirm beyond any doubt the right of the individual to a healthy life. It should be left to the executives to find ways and means of ensuring this. . . . What is both necessary and desirable is the association and cooperation of those without property to enable them to face the ranks of those who have, so that ultimately men will no longer be machines of other men.[37]

He ended:

> These are radical measures which I suggest as remedies to prevent the return of famine and a vast typhoid epidemic. Those who are unable to appreciate the dynamics of cultural history may find them far-fetched but those who are sufficiently clear-headed as to be able to understand our present situation can only agree with me. In the final analysis every individual has the right of existence and health, and the state is responsible for ensuring this.[38]

As Howard Waitzkin points out, for Virchow the sources of disease were poverty and unemployment, political disenfranchisement and lack of education.[39] Recognizing the unequal distribution of disease, Virchow saw its fundamental cause in unequal access to society's products.

Engels, in contrast, defined the social etiology of disease somewhat differently. He also linked disease to poverty and unemployment, but he assigned primary responsibility to the political economy. Engels's contribution to the idea that disease is caused by social conditions is entirely contained in his 1845 treatise "The Condition of the Working Class in England."[40] Writing about "social misery" in general, he emphasized disease in particular. Widespread, unremitting disease is, after all, one of the two classic signposts of an unjust society, the other being constant rebellion. Like Edwin Chadwick and most of the social reformers of his day, Engels believed that miasmas carry disease. ("The filth and stagnant pools of the working people's quarters in the great cities have . . . the worst effect upon the public health, because they produce precisely those gases which engender disease; so, too, the exhalations from contaminated streams.")[41] His descriptions of slum conditions are virtually indistinguishable from Chadwick's portrayals in *The Report on the Sanitary Condition of the Labouring Population of Great Britain* published three years earlier.[42] Indeed, Engels refers to Chadwick. Both men were appalled at the filth, crowding, and despair, and both emphasized the danger to health from disgusting smells. Unlike Chadwick, however, Engels looked beyond the cesspools and the garbage. Behind them, so to speak, he saw a particular kind of economic production and called it the true cause of disease.

Although in his more polemical passages, Engels personified causality ("A pretty list of diseases engendered purely by the hateful money-greed of the manufacturers! Women made unfit for child-bearing, children deformed, men enfeebled, limbs crushed, whole generations wrecked, afflicted with disease and infirmity, purely to fill the purses of the bourgeoisie"),[43] in general, he blamed the English production system. With some reservations he agreed that better working conditions would "increase the cost of production and incapacitate the English producers for competition in foreign markets, and [cause] wages [to] fall."[44] But, he continued, all of this proves "nothing except this, that the industrial greatness of England can be maintained only through the barbarous treatment of the operatives, the destruction of their health, the social, physical, and mental decay of whole generations."[45]

He made a similar analysis of slum life. The overcrowding, the fetid air, the open sewers, the lack of food made people sick: "How is it possible, under such conditions, for the lower class to be healthy and long lived? What else can be expected than an excessive mortality, an unbroken series of epidemics, a progressive deterioration in the physique of the working population?"[46] But the fundamental cause was a system of production based on competition. Drawing on Adam Smith and Thomas Malthus, Engels argued that when both the workers and the bourgeoisie are in competition among themselves, great swings of prosperity and poverty inevitably result:[47]

> If there are too few labourers on hand, prices, i.e., wages, rise, the workers are more prosperous, marriages multiply, more children are born and more live to grow up, until a sufficient number of labourers has been secured. If there are too many on hand, prices fall, want of work, poverty, and starvation, and consequent diseases arise, and the "surplus population" is put out of the way. . . . These starving workers are then removed from the market, they can buy nothing, and the quantity of articles of consumption previously required by them is no longer in demand, need no longer be produced; the workers previously employed in producing them are therefore driven out of work, and are also removed from the market, and so it goes on, always the same old round.[48]

In their different ways, both Engels and Virchow tried to tie disease to phenomena that seem existentially removed from the concrete experience of fever, cough, vomit, rash, diarrhea, and pain. Instead of locating the primary cause as close as possible to the personal experience of sickness, they placed it as far away as possible. Their views made disease prevention a matter of social change. This kind of reasoning, of course, is always disquieting, for it cannot help but call into question the government and the system of production. Since in any society most people usually believe they have more to lose than to gain from major political and economic change, disease causality analyses of this nature get shunted off to the periphery of legitimate thought. Aiding the marginalization of Virchow's and Engels's way of thinking, the germ theory of disease causality and an individualist conception of human society gradually became the dominant framework within which people thought about illness. It was not until the political upheavals of the last third of the twentieth century that a social analysis of disease causality found its way into the disease prevention literature again.

In the last fifteen years a group of radical thinkers—intellectual descendants of Virchow and Engels—have argued for a new linear model of disease causality, one that turns the old germ theory–based model upsidedown. In their view, microparticles are the last cause of disease, while first place goes to the social system. This is the ultimate environmental theory. It makes most disease an artifact of unjust social systems. Mainstream policy proposals, these thinkers say, limited by the assumption that extant political and economic structures are inviolable, can only be partially effective. It is by looking critically at the social roots of disease that effective prevention policies will be developed. As Meredith Turshen puts it, "health and disease are products of the way society is organized, of the way subsistence is produced as well as surplus, and of the way subsistence and surplus are distributed among the members of society. . . . The consequences for prevention and cure that follow from this theory of disease are the need for fundamental social reorganization."[49] And Evan Stark says, "From the standpoint of this new epidemiology, the central question is not what makes people sick, but whether the social irrationalities from which disease arises on a mass scale are any longer based on the limits of human development."[50]

One of the more ambitious attempts to describe disease causality from this perspective is Joseph Eyer and Peter Sterling's linkage of mortality with specific features of modern life in capitalist countries, including unemployment, lack of community, and high-pressure work.[51] Drawing on a wide variety of demographic data, they argue that "the economic and cultural forces in capitalist society create chronic stress [and early death] by (1) disrupting attempts to reestablish communal ties, and (2) molding competitive, striving people who find it difficult to build these ties even when external forces of disruption are removed."[52]

Working from a similar perspective, Peter Schnall and Rochelle Kern review the research that correlates hypertension with social class, occupation, race, age, and gender.[53] They conclude that most such studies "presented these variables as if they were characteristics of individuals rather than reflections of patterns of society." A more effective epidemiology, they argue, would

> examine these correlations and categories *simultaneously* in order to identify the broad social and physical context in which hypertension occurs. Social class, occupation, race, age, and gender are interrelated in the organization of society. The political economy of capitalism (with its particular social and cultural characteristics) gives rise to both the organization of American society and the distribution and patterns of diseases within it.[54]

Most critics of mainstream explanations for disease examine the connection between work and health. Robert Karasek, for instance, has studied jobs that are hectic and psychologically demanding and that give workers little freedom to make decisions.[55] He finds a positive correlation between these high-demand/low-control jobs and coronary heart disease and suggests that the issue is not merely redesigning jobs but understanding "the reasons why job design as currently practiced results in such large numbers of workers with excessive job demands and insufficient job control."[56] More forthrightly, Vicente Navarro traces poor health to unequal access to political and economic power. In his contribution to a volume on the political economy of work and health, he sums up this position: "the fight for the realization of health is very much at the center of the conflict between capital and labor which takes place at the workplace and heightens in moments of crisis like the current one."[57]

By and large, the work of these critics has three major weaknesses. First, by assigning responsibility to capitalism, most of them ignore the presence of disease in precapitalist and socialist countries. They would have the history of disease begin in the late eighteenth century with the Industrial Revolution and take place only in some parts of the world. Second, many of them express themselves in clichés. They choose words and phrases so encumbered with stale political thinking that not only do the critics themselves seem unreflective but important readers refuse to reflect on their interpretations. Dismissed out of hand by most of the people who have the power to put their suggestions into practice, the critics are left talking only to one another. Third, their tendency to think and write about abstractions makes verification by other scholars difficult. Eyer and Sterling, for example, subsume the unhealthy characteristics of capitalist society under the term *stress,* a concept even more resistant to empirical investigation than the phenomena it represents. And Karasek's definitions of control and demand are quite job specific. In other words, the whole perspective badly needs refinement. Nevertheless for the purpose of disease prevention, the perspective is intriguing because, by refusing to treat the status quo as sacred, it points the way to effective policies. Its champions trace disease not to microscopic agents nor to personal action nor to a great web that includes these factors among many others. Instead, they trace it to more fundamental causes: political and economic decisions and beliefs that result in an unequal distribution of power and resources, in exposures to harmful substances, in poor diets, and in unhealthy behavior. In essence, they say that policy analysts should begin by assuming that disease originates in the social structure.

The idea that the social structure causes disease is not foreign to Americans. Most of us easily see it generating diseases in cultures we have reason to criticize. Thus even the popular press in the United States analyzes alcoholism in the Soviet Union or malnutrition in South Africa in terms of those countries' political ideologies and economic institutions. People drink excessively in the USSR, the newspaper and magazine articles insinuate, because they are unhappy or bored, and they feel that way because the Soviet system generates despair and monotony. Or, people are malnourished in South Africa because apartheid fosters poverty. By the same token, we are accustomed to noting structural causes for infectious diseases in the Third World. The persistence of these diseases seems to be neither a medical nor a personal problem; these obviously are diseases of poverty. The people who get them are the poor. You do not find much yellow fever or cholera or typhus or polio among middle- and upper-class people in Guatemala, Somalia, and the Philippines. This is because these people have decent sanitation, adequate nutrition, modern medical care, good education, secure employment, and regular leisure. They have them as a result of being well-off.

In contrast, both the popular and academic press tend to explain the persistence of disease in contemporary America—not only alcoholism and malnutrition, but cardiovascular diseases and cancers as well—in individual terms. As I showed in chapter two, explanations run from those on a molecular level to proposals that people get sick because they make bad choices.[58] Despite the clarity of the relation between disease and the social structure in other times and places, we are uncomfortable making definite causal associations between *our* major diseases and an unequal distribution of wealth and power. Instead of calling these factors the fundamental causes of diseases in our country today, most of us welcome the chance to dilute the effect of politics and economics on disease in a complex "multicausal" analysis.

But poverty, to take one example of a fundamental cause, plays the same role here as in the Third World. Compared with the poor, the upper and middle classes breathe cleaner air, live farther from industrial plants and toxic waste sites, work at healthier jobs, have more control over their lives and thus less stress, have greater access to preventive medicine, are better educated, and, partly because they benefit more from governmental policies and economic decisions, are more likely to listen when authorities advise them not to smoke (see Figure 1, in chap. two). In other words, these healthy things are related to their class position.

From this it would follow that reducing poverty is as important a strategy for addressing disease now as it was in the nineteenth century. Moreover it seems to make as much sense for industrial countries as it does for nonindustrial ones. Specifically, this line of thinking implies that the people most likely to become sick—the lower classes—need to live in social and physical environments more like those of the people less likely to become sick—the upper classes. The multifactorial view of disease tries, I think, to support this idea. So does the environmental perspective. But neither lends itself well to proposals for social change. Or, more accurately perhaps, each can readily be used to avoid making significant changes. The multicausal theory dances around the problem of a causal hierarchy; the environmental theory threatens to plunge back to the reductionist germ and lifestyle theories. In contrast, the structural proposal provides a starting place for the kind of disease prevention policy that was so successful in the nineteenth century.

For one thing, it says that disease prevention need not be tackled head on. Whatever makes life better in general also makes it healthier. So the provision of decent housing, good schools, and satisfying jobs would be a prime means of preventing disease. More specifically, the structural perspective directs prevention first to the interaction between government and industry. For the control of environmental toxins, for example, it would not just say that disease prevention requires stricter and better enforced laws regulating hazardous processes and products; it would ask for a different relationship among government, citizens, and industry. A perspective that focused on this relationship, instead of on industries' products or wastes, would shift the emphasis away from the regulation of individual toxins. Instead it would concentrate on the lack of democratic participation in production decisions. It might suggest that citizens should have a voice in what things get produced, how they get produced, and what substances the production processes utilize. Judging from the proposals of environmental groups, more democratic decision making would likely change the current policies that give companies licenses to emit specific pollutants into the air and water and that legalize toxic exposures of workers. A structural view also might say that the workday should be designed so that employees can get physical exercise and release from stress and that commercial advertisers should be discouraged from promoting unhealthy diets.

The strength of the structural perspective is twofold. First, it does not mistake political and economic systems for natural objects. They become amenable to redress. Thus policy makers adopting the structural perspective need not limit themselves to disease prevention proposals that preserve the current distribution of power. They need not compromise prevention possibilities at the outset by omitting those that do not fit into the status quo. Second, for the most part, the policies it suggests benefit a whole population, not just certain individuals in it. While certain diseases are not, in fact, explicable in term of the social structure—Alzheimer's, multiple sclerosis, and Huntington's chorea for example—a search for causality that begins at the social level and only moves later to secondary levels guards against unwittingly developing limited policies.

The structural perspective thus appears to fulfill the criteria for a better conception of disease causality. Unlike the multicausal theory, it identifies a fundamental cause of disease, thereby providing a starting place for prevention proposals. Unlike the germ, lifestyle, and environmental theories, it guards against reductionist thinking, and it includes nonempirical aspects of causality. It does, however, have two apparent disadvantages: it seems to imply that the reduction of morbidity and mortality must wait on major social change and that disease prevention must be impersonal.

Consider its application in the toxic waste issue. A truly effective public health policy aimed at preventing exposure to these chemicals would concern itself with stemming the production of wastes. Such a policy might offer solutions like recycling, substitution, and neutralization. In the meantime, however, something must be done with the stuff on hand, so policies concerned with the siting of hazardous waste dumps or the development of alternative disposal technologies must be acceptable as stopgap measures. Take another example: control of AIDS in intravenous drug users. A structural perspective would concentrate on ending heroin addiction. It would ask why large numbers of people are in such despair that they turn to drugs, and would propose social changes to address the despair. But distributing free, clean needles to addicts is immediately effective, at least for those who get them. The policy reduces the AIDS problem to dirty needles rather than expanding it to the social conditions that engender drug addiction. But it is better than doing nothing.

In its second apparent disadvantage, the structural perspective on disease causality seems to say that there is little that individual men and women can do to protect themselves from illness. As such, the theory resembles the multicausal one, which also offers no guidance for action. But it is not quite the same thing. The multicausal theory lacks guidelines for *policy makers*, whereas the structural view lacks guidelines for *individuals*. We often need, it seems, personal policies that are different from public ones. We need to know what interim, individual actions we can rely on until public policies are in place. As long as workplaces are unhealthy; as long as toxins contaminate the food and water, air and soil; as long as unhealthy behavior is socially rewarded or difficult to avoid—then it would verge on the suicidal to advocate only prevention policies that require someone else to take action.

Take the case of rape prevention. Progress has been slow, but at least most public policy makers are willing to agree now that social and political factors evinced in the objectification of women, not the personal behavior of women, constitute the fundamental cause of rape. Acknowledging that if women's behavior is considered the cause, then women become not only the victims but also the perpetrators of rape, the populace is gradually understanding that women's low social status accounts significantly for rape and that other presumed causes such as pornography and women's behavior are primarily themselves consequences of that low status. Therefore rape can be decreased by the myriad changes that make women full members of society, instead of mainly helpmates of one sort or another and producers of children.

Now that is all very enlightened, but it does not help the woman who has to walk down deserted streets at night nor the woman caught in a relationship with a violent man. She needs a *personal* rape prevention policy. For her, it is important to know that some behavior change, or some environmental change—more street lights, maybe—may prevent rape. Without that knowledge, she is a potential victim twice over, once of rape and once of a sexist society.

The lifestyle theory of disease causality presents another example. It is less clear-cut, for except in the case of cigarette smoking, its elements are less surely linked to disease prevention than to physical fitness. Nevertheless, we can, as individuals, definitely reduce our chances of heart disease and cancer if we do not smoke. If we change our diets and take up exercise, we may possibly reduce our chances even more. Changes in the availability of cigarettes, nutritious food, and exercise would have a wider social impact; but individual change helps individuals. Similarly, for people who work around toxic substances, the most effective disease prevention program would clean up the occupational environment; but in the meantime, workers need to know that respirators, special clothing, and other personal devices may fairly well protect them. If personal actions can effectively prevent disease or other unwanted events, then people should know about them.

But, as I have been arguing, a *public* health policy that consists mainly of exhorting individuals to change their behavior appears at best to be shortsighted. At worst it seems less a policy directed at attaining health for the public than one bent on protecting the institutions (whether they are sexism, particular workplaces, or the political economy itself) threatening that health. The issue, however, may be more complicated. If advocates of personal prevention hope for really effective disease prevention, they do have a responsibility to prescribe social prevention as preeminent and to put individual action in a context that indicates its surrogate role. The very notion that individual people can be conceptually separated from the society in which they live needs examination. In other words, the individual–social dichotomy itself is questionable. The next chapter takes up this problem.

CHAPTER 4

Cuba and Health Promotion

In all three of the preceding chapters, I have criticized theories of disease causality that place major responsibility for prevention on individuals and have looked with a certain amount of favor on theories that identify broader entities—the environment, the society, or the social structure—as causal. I have, in other words, assumed that it is possible to separate conceptually individuals from their social and environmental contexts. It is not an unusual assumption. Every question about apportioning responsibility for health between the individual and the society begins from this dualistic presupposition. So do questions about the desirability of social change versus the desirability of personal change. In the case of cigarette smoking, for example, some policy analysts ask whether the policy emphasis should be on getting people to stop smoking or whether it should be on making social and cultural change so cigarettes are not as available, or promoted, or needed. Those on the left usually favor social change. They tend to oppose health education programs that put all the responsibility on individuals. But posing the issue this way may be part of the problem. It takes for granted a dichotomy between the individual and the society that, however embedded in western thinking, may be more an artifact of modernism than a representation of reality.

This chapter examines the distinction between individual and social responsibility for health. It is the first of three chapters presenting cases where hidden arguments influence our ideas about disease prevention. Here the issue is approached the long way around. I begin with a fairly detailed description of health education in Cuba and go from there to a consideration of the dualistic assumptions behind most American criticism of individual responsibility for health.

In the United States, advocates of the lifestyle theory of disease causality call health education the best means of reducing cardiovascular disease and cancer. Health promotion, as it is called, has been for many years the disease prevention policy most favored by the U.S. government. Critics of the lifestyle theory point both to its conservative bias and to its lack of efficacy. Since it refuses to call attention to structural causes of disease, it tacitly supports the very relationships and institutions that produce disease in the first place. Many of these critics imply that in a less capitalistic, liberal, bourgeois society, health education would be different. Instead of urging people to make individual efforts aimed at overcoming the unhealthy environments in which they live—to swim upstream, so to speak—health education would primarily be a force for changing unhealthy physical and social environments. Such education would focus on the economic and political determinants of disease. Some critics have even suggested that it would interpret all disease as an indicator of an unjust or improperly organized society. To the extent that nonbourgeois health education did call for individual change, that change would be part of a process of politicization. It would teach people to conceive of disease causality in political and economic, not individual, terms. Health education would empower people to take into their own hands the social change necessary for healthful lives.[1] This is a provocative critique. It castigates not health education per se, but a particular kind of health education: that which calls only for individual change.

The suggestion that socialist societies design different kinds of health education programs drew me to Cuba.[2] Taking my cue from the literature critical of the lifestyle theory and of health education in the United States, I wanted to learn whether Cubans make disease prevention a social responsibility. In that socialist society does health education call for social change, or does it rely on individual change? Does it emphasize environmental sources of disease? Does it seek to empower people not just to make changes in their own lives but to bring about the necessary social changes that would make the society more healthy for everyone?

I was in Cuba for only two weeks, and although I spent almost the entire time conducting formal and informal interviews, my answers to these questions are necessarily tentative. They are even possibly out of date, since my visit took place in 1984. Nevertheless they do challenge some assumptions about the differences between socialist and capitalist societies. The superficial answers are as follows: Health education in Cuba does not call for social change, nor does it emphasize environmental sources of disease. Health education there, at least that aimed at the prevention of chronic disease, appears to promote individual change. It does seek to empower people, but not in order to make fundamental social change. Such blunt statements need elaboration, and the rest of this chapter develops these claims, providing examples, and adding caveats. More important, it tries to put Cuban policy in a Cuban context. It shows that the very way that I and many other American critics pose the issue fails to recognize a fundamental difference between Cuba and the United States: the two cultures celebrate decidedly different relationships between the individual and the society.

Cuban Health Promotion

Before the 1959 revolution, Cuba was typical of underdeveloped countries in that life expectancy at birth was low (58 years in 1959), infant mortality was high (70 deaths per 1,000 live births), infectious disease mortality was similarly high (94.4 per 1,000 people), and diarrheal diseases were a major cause of death.[3] The new government immediately put great emphasis on improving health. They created the Ministry of Public Health (MINSAP) with responsibility for all matters pertaining to health, from medical schools through the production of pharmaceuticals to environmental sanitation. They trained thousands of new physicians and built primary care clinics (called *policlinics*) and hospitals throughout the country in order to give the entire population access to good medical care. In addition they created block organizations called Committees for the Defense of the Revolution (CDRs) in every city, town, and village. Virtually everyone in the country belongs to a CDR, and these organizations include among their activities responsibility for such health-related tasks as neighborhood sanitation and inoculation against infectious diseases.

Besides these acts, the new government tore down thousands of slum dwellings and moved people to adequate housing. They rationed and drastically reduced the price of essential foods to guarantee everyone basic nutrition. They initiated countrywide literacy campaigns. They practically wiped out unemployment. They educated thousands of new teachers and made all schooling free.[4] These and other changes (e.g., improvement in the status of women, a major land reform project, better roads and communication), albeit instituted with many setbacks, mistakes, and problems, caused a dramatic change in morbidity and mortality. Life expectancy has risen to seventy-three years, and today Cubans point with a mixture of pride and irony to the fact that cardiovascular diseases and cancer are the major causes of death.[5]

It is important to note that when Cubans report on health (see any of Fidel Castro's speeches to the people), they describe medical services, not the broad social actions that the above paragraph implies are responsible for improvements in morbidity and mortality. Observers in this country have frequently remarked that MINSAP, dominated by physicians, advances a view of health that roots it in medical care, despite the data showing that medical care has only secondary influence on the health of any population.[6] Such a stance reflects and perpetuates a mechanical model of health and disease and thus individualizes illness.[7]

The reader may not be surprised, then, to learn that to prevent chronic diseases, MINSAP relies mainly on health promotion (*promoción de salud*). To Americans this has a familiar ring.

Health promotion in Cuba means getting regular exercise and stopping smoking. It is a fight, I was told over and over, against three "bad habits": sedentariness, obesity, and smoking. The entire program relies on persuading people to change their behavior. "This is our major emphasis in health education," the head of one policlinic told me. "This is a national campaign to bring to the person better knowledge about the dangers of bad habits, to show individuals what they can do to improve their health."[8]

These projects are the responsibility of the national office of health education, a section within MINSAP, headed by Dr. Jorge Borroto, a large, enthusiastic man who was a dentist in private practice before the revolution. His office, of course, carries on a variety of other health education projects besides the fight against bad habits.[9] Newest among them are a vigorous sex education campaign aimed at reducing the rising number of adolescent pregnancies, an occupational safety and health campaign, and a small campaign to reduce traffic accidents, the major cause of death among young people. In all the campaigns, the element of personal responsibility predominates.

The campaign against sedentariness, obesity, and smoking began in early 1981 and at the beginning concentrated almost exclusively on obesity and sedentariness. A 1983 booklet written for the Ministry of Culture by a member of MINSAP's Commission on Health Promotion explains the program:

> In our country, close to 40% of the deaths are caused by cardiovascular diseases. . . . We must keep in mind that our way of life is a determining factor and that it is up to us to decrease the high incidence of diabetes, obesity, arterial hypertension and heart attacks. . . . [S]edentariness, obesity and the bad habit of smoking are important risk factors in the development of cardiovascular diseases. The people who suffer from high blood pressure, obesity, elevated concentrations of cholesterol in the blood, or a combination of these factors, run greater risks of death from cardiovascular diseases than people who are not fat, who have normal blood pressure and low concentrations of blood cholesterol.
>
> Recently, there has been much interest in the possible role of systematic physical exercise in the genesis of these diseases. Some authors have stressed the importance of systematic physical

exercise as a general factor in cardiovascular health. In many young people less than twenty years old, one can find the first signs of arteriosclerotic changes in the blood vessels, but if these changes do not reach an advanced stage, they can be reversed, which is why we urge a modification of lifestyle through the incorporation of systematic exercising as an element of health promotion.[10]

The rest of the health promotion campaign is so similar to the one in the United States that Americans who run everyday, or who work out in gymnasiums, would feel right at home in Cuba. I saw somewhat fewer people jogging in Havana than I would expect to see on summer days in a U.S. city of two million people, but I was repeatedly told that the number has steadily grown. Running shoes are ubiquitous, worn not only by runners but, it seems, by every teenager in town. In an extension of the emphasis on sports, decommercialized and heavily promoted, that took place after the revolution, the state regularly sponsors races including a yearly marathon. Every neighborhood has a high school, and nearly every high school has a gymnasium and a playing field. These are available to the community before and after school hours.[11]

The exercise campaign, of course, meets resistance in some quarters. Trying to overcome the reluctance of people to participate, the booklet quoted above proposes that running is a mark of sophistication:

> Remember that it is fundamental to change our customs. Often we are timid about starting exercises and we look for excuses: that it's not proper because of our age or our social position. "Well I, a serious person, can hardly be expected to put on shorts and a T-shirt and run around the streets and parks of the city!" But don't be shy. We are sure that the time will come when the intellectual level of a man will be determined not only by how well he does in his profession, if he reads a lot, if he writes, if he knows how to act in society, if he understands music, etc., but also by his consciousness of the necessity of systematic exercises.[12]

Along with a certain lack of enthusiasm, Cubans frequently express the same irreverence, the same sort of ridicule, that many Americans do about exercising. For example, speaking to a national conference of the CDRs in October 1981, Castro amused everyone by beginning on this ironic note: "A brief incidental matter: don't worry if you see me walking with a bit of difficulty—although I believe I walked straight—because in trying to carry on the fight against sedentariness and obesity [and here the audience began to laugh] I was working out and managed to break a small bone in the toe of my right foot."[13]

The Cuban exercise campaign contains another, somewhat more salient similarity to the one in the United States. Like the U.S. campaign this one avoids suggesting that the workplace be reorganized to include regular opportunities for physical exercise. Significantly, it acknowledges frequently that the mode of production has a causal relationship to mortality. The booklet that equates exercise with intellectual life says: "In general, working conditions in modern life are characterized by a progressive elimination of physical effort. . . . This lack creates special conditions in the human organism. . . . Modern man must understand that to preserve his health, he needs to take up a systematic program of physical exercise."[14] A small pamphlet promoting walking makes the same point: "The constant development of civilization supplies man with machines that partly reduce the physical effort he has to employ in other times in his daily work. [Thus] the practice of systematic walks is useful as an activity to prevent cardiovascular disease."[15] Another pamphlet, this one devoted to sit-up exercises, echoes the theme:

> The natural movements of daily life are not sufficient for the perfect regulation of our organism. Scientific and technical developments have simplified man's physical activity, encouraging a sedentary way of life that carries with it poorly functioning organs and systems that affect the general state of health. Physical exercises, practiced systematically, are capable of preventing, arresting, and eliminating a high percentage of disorders and diseases.[16]

In other words, the policy of physical activity to ward off cardiovascular diseases acknowledges the basis of disease in the mode of production but does not discuss this contradiction between production and health. The policy simply states that the Cuban economy causes disease and then blandly proposes that people must take it upon themselves to overcome the inherently unhealthy economy.

Since this attitude so closely resembles the official U.S. position, one might ask why it deserves mention. Every economic system seems to be unhealthy in some regard; before Cuba was socialist, its citizens suffered the diseases of undeveloped capitalism. Disease, many argue, is merely a question of tradeoffs. With economic development comes chronic disease. The best we can do is hope that. people will resist the diseases and behavior the system engenders. Indeed this viewpoint appears to govern health education policy in Cuba. If so, however, it deserves considerable attention because it directly conflicts with a principle central to Marxism. Underpinning all socialist ideology is the maxim that people's social, political, and intellectual lives stem from their society's mode of production. Marx explained it in a much-quoted passage:

> In the social production of their life, men enter into definite relations that are indispensable and independent of their will, relations of production which correspond to a definite stage of development of their material productive forces. The sum total of these relations of production constitutes the economic structure of society, on which rises a legal and political superstructure and to which correspond definite forms of social consciousness. The mode of production of material life conditions the social, political, and intellectual life process in general. It is not the consciousness of men that determines their behavior, but, on the contrary, their social being that determines their consciousness.[17]

It is a complex observation, not to be interpreted, most Marxists agree, to mean that economics *determine* behavior, for what Marx called "mode of production" combines two other elaborate concepts: the *means* of production (material, skills, techniques, and the population available to use them) and *relations* of production (social classes and institutions of power). So there is a dialectical relation among the elements of society: people create and are created by their institutions. The point here, however, is that in direct contrast to the bourgeois supposition that ideas and social institutions are the foundation of economic life, in the Marxist view, it is economic life that gives rise to ideas and sows the seeds of social structure. Or, as Czech writer Jakub Netoplik puts it, "The modification of the way of life is only possible through the modification of the conditions of life."[18]

Marx did not write directly about health, but clearly disease prevention policy and health promotion practices fall under the rubric of social, political, and intellectual life. Thus from a Marxist standpoint, health behavior is a reflection of underlying economic institutions and cannot be effectively changed without changing the mode of production that produced them. So it seems that the current Cuban policy for combating sedentariness and obesity runs counter to what should be Cuba's own principles. Certainly it contraposes Marxist wisdom about where to begin making effective change. In the face of chronic diseases, Cubans have apparently taken precisely the stance adopted by complacent Americans about our country: since we have a basically well-designed society, only personal and psychological problems remain. In other words, Cubans appear to have embraced exactly the same end-of-ideology position that, despite the upheavals of the Vietnam era, characterizes most American opinion. In fact, the Ministry of Culture captures this sentiment in the preface to its booklet on running: "The Revolution allows us to add more years to our life," it says, evidently referring to the control of infectious diseases and malnutrition; "now it is up to us to add more life to those years."[19] In other words, one cannot expect the revolution to do anything about chronic diseases. These are personal problems.

Is this an accurate interpretation of Cuban policy? Before attempting an answer, it is worthwhile to look at the health promotion campaign to reduce smoking as well as at the incipient health education programs aimed at occupational diseases and traffic accidents.

No-Smoking Campaign

Per capita cigarette consumption in Cuba is third highest in the world, right after Cyprus and Greece.[20] Until 1983, however, MINSAP's antismoking policy consisted mainly of printing warnings on cigarette packages ("Smoking damages your health"). The new policy, lagging some two years behind the rest of the health promotion campaign, takes a more vigorous stand against smoking. Thus for the first time Cubans have a strong program that might reduce lung cancer. At least that is how Americans would define the goal. The Cuban Ministry of Public Health, however, is not publicly worried about cancer. Virtually everyone I talked with equated smoking, not with cancer, but with damage to the heart. Exhortation to stop smoking evidently means to most Cubans protection against heart attacks. This is a reasonable emphasis, given that, like Americans, many more Cubans die from cardiovascular diseases than from cancers.

Like the fight against sedentariness and obesity, the fight against smoking relies entirely on voluntary behavior change. "The state has not come to the drastic point of forbidding cigarettes," I was told in one meeting at a Havana policlinic. "That would be very violent. We have propaganda campaigns about the damage that cigarettes do, and we give people enough information to arrive at their own decisions. Our primary objective is that people themselves should know that smoking is dangerous." The policlinic's health educator continued: "Everyone knows now about the health hazards of smoking. A hundred percent of the population is very clear on this. But," she smiled a bit wearily, "as in all parts of the world, they don't pay attention. You have to feel the threat of a heart attack to pay attention."

No-smoking campaigns are always based on assumptions about why people smoke in the first place. In the United States, health educators offer one or more of the following explanations for smoking. They note the seductive advertising that equates smoking with good times, sexual prowess, sophistication, and physical fitness;[21] they point to social pressure, especially among young people, for whom smoking signals maturity and experience;[22] they assume that people smoke because they do not know it is dangerous;[23] they consider the economic aspects, directing attention to price supports for the tobacco industry;[24] they show how cigarette smoking fills a psychological need to reduce the stress people experience in their daily lives;[25] finally, many point out that tobacco is physically addicting.[26] Each of these explanations confers accountability for smoking on a different group of people, and the resulting political argument over responsibility is far from settled. No one theory yet predominates here.

In Cuba there seems to be no political debate about causality. The first of these theories is completely inappropriate (neither cigarettes nor any other product is advertised), and MINSAP, at least publicly, disregards the economic, psychological, and physiological arguments. Instead it advances the educational and social arguments. The no-smoking campaign reflects an implicit assumption that smoking is mostly just a bad habit and that social pressure, poor role models, and lack of education play the predominant role in perpetuating it.

Personnel at MINSAP consistently preface "smoking" with "the bad habit of," thus designating it superficial behavior, a custom people can do something about if they just put their minds to it. When I asked Dr. Borroto, the national director of health education, what his office was doing about cigarette smoking, he answered:

> Well, we are informing people. In the first place, the doctor can't smoke. If the doctor smokes we won't win the battle. We just won't win the battle. And there are many physicians in Cuba who smoke, young physicians and old physicians, but now the ministry says they can't smoke in front of patients and they're complying pretty well. We're going to begin a program very soon to get support from the mass organizations to take up a big fight against the bad habit of smoking. In Cuba there is a problem. We are producers of tobacco, and it's a good tobacco, and there is a lot of transmission of smoking from the grandfather to the father to the son. So it's not easy to break. Well, now we're beginning to work. You have to start with young children. We're starting programs in the schools, on TV, etc. You have to *educate* the population about the habit of smoking. It's more than just prohibiting smoking in certain places. Fortunately, we don't have any problem with the tobacco transnationals. That's an advantage we have. There are no ads on TV.

The health educator of one Havana policlinic described the program in similiar terms: "You know how Fidel always appeared with a big cigar? Well, now he doesn't. I don't think he's stopped smoking, but he doesn't smoke on TV any more. He announced once that he wouldn't smoke and since then we haven't seen him with a cigar in his hand."[27] She went on, "We have an agreement with the radio and the TV, and they try to eliminate cigarettes and ostentatious smoking. On TV the heroes don't smoke now, only the villains. In the policlinics there's no smoking. And the teachers in school can't smoke. But in the universities the professors still smoke. We still have lots of problems. But of course the campaign is only one year old." How long it will continue, what new forms it will take, and how successful it will be are topics for further investigation. But at this point, it seems unlikely that the economic explanation for smoking will ever predominate. I brought it up with Dr. Borroto: "What about the contradiction, that we also have, between the production of tobacco and a no-smoking campaign?" His answer:

> Well, yes, we have said that Cuba would like to suspend the production of tobacco. But how can we sacrifice tobacco production if we don't have anything to substitute for it on the international market? What will take the place of all the revenue?[28] It is very elegant to say it [that we'll stop production], but what answers do we give to the international market, to the FAO [Food and Agriculture Organization], etc.? Besides, Cuban tobacco has worldwide prestige. We're fighting against the bad habit of smoking. As doctors we know that smoking is bad and the government provides a program of activities to combat it.

Occupational Safety and Health

A brief remark about occupational safety and health in Cuba: it follows the same pattern. Workers learn how to use personal devices to protect themselves from toxins, not how to recognize dangerous substances on the job, not how to rid the workplace of possible health hazards, not how to press for more protective laws or regulations. Moreover, if workers fail to use the respirators, the earplugs, or the other safety devices deemed necessary, the ministry fines them. Fines range from five to fifty pesos, depending on the severity of the infraction (although MINSAP was considering lowering fines), and the fines are taken out of a worker's pocket, not simply (and less dramatically) deducted from her or his pay.[29]

"We are not as developed in occupational health education as we are in the health education for the masses," said Dr. Graciela Solis, director of health education for the city of Havana.

> We're still working on this. It's not as good as it should be. We already have nurses and doctors in the factories, and they are studying the problem in order to learn its magnitude. You know that health education is everyone's task, but one also needs to have someone who controls, and who supervises, to convince and persuade. Since many physicians are afraid of it, and others are not convinced of the importance of health education, we have begun this work. In occupational medicine, then, what are we doing? Well, it's very little. But, for example, there's often a radio in the workplace that plays music and messages about fundamental personal hygiene—that you ought to wash your hands before eating, things like that, no? Well, we also do that in face-to-face discussions. The nurses are in the workplace every Saturday, and they show slides and movies about such things as eye diseases, or silicoses, or noise. They ask [pedagogic] questions about why we should wear hard hats, and etc. They also try to prevent, try to learn the reasons for accidents. In addition, we have psychologists doing research to learn what the psychological effect is of a lot of noise, for example, or of having to make very fast movements, or of having very monotonous work.

Currently the state publishes no official records on occupational disease. Like the United States until recently, Cuba publishes figures only about occupational injuries, something far more tractable. The policlinic structure is now being augmented to include separate occupational medicine clinics (the first, in Cienfuegos, opened in 1984), and these should help to yield better statistics. The new clinics may turn out to be part of an occupational health program far more effective than ours, because clinical, surveillance, and regulatory activities are all part of the same institute. But as Dr. Solis noted, the current program is in its infancy. The Ministry of Public Health is trying to increase the number of occupational health personnel and is working on the formation of explicit standards, adapted to Cuba's climate, for more occupational exposures. At present, most of the standards are for physical factors like noise, vibration, ventilation, and lighting.[30] It remains to be seen whether the policy to reduce occupational disease will continue to put so much onus on workers themselves to change to more healthy behavior.

TRAFFIC ACCIDENTS

Given this information on the policies for reducing chronic diseases, it is reasonable to predict that Cuba's efforts to reduce traffic fatalities are also seemingly based on a your-fault assumption. And so they are. Granted that automobile collisions might have low priority in a country emphasizing mass transportation over private automobiles, nevertheless, deaths from traffic accidents increase every year.[31] In the United States, progressives in this field argue that the focus should not be on preventing accidents but on preventing injuries. Concentrating on the former, they point out, leads mainly to driver education, whereas concentrating on the latter shifts attention to the design of cars and roads—social, not personal, considerations. Although they are concerned with, say, getting drunk drivers off the streets and highways, progressives here are more interested in passive restraints than in safe driving rules.[32] In Cuba, however, the focus is on accidents, not injuries, and the source of the problem is unambiguously located at the individual level.

Says a Cuban booklet titled *Popular Health Themes*:

> The most frequent traffic accidents are the run-over, the collision, and the overturn. In these accidents, the human factor represents the most important causal element, making adequate education the best method of prevention. This education ought to begin at the very youngest age and be reinforced in the school. Children ought to know and comply with traffic regulations as pedestrians. We must offer drivers adequate training and must educate them

in the norms of conduct in the socialist society so they will carry with them at all times a respect for the traffic rules, to avoid accidents that represent losses of good material and the most important: the life of man."

Seat belts are not only rarely mentioned in Cuba; they frequently do not even exist. Certainly they do not adorn the many pre-1959 American cars that still chug faithfully along the streets, nor are they always features of the new cars (mostly Eastern European) that predominate. I never saw anyone use a seat belt during my visit to Cuba, and when I once struggled to disentangle one in a physician's car, she dismissed the problem with a wave of her hand: "We don't make people do that here."

It was similar to the remark I had heard earlier that the state would never prohibit cigarettes: "That would be very violent. We give people enough education to arrive at their own decisions." It is also, of course, virtually identical to the position held by political conservatives in the United States: just provide the facts and let people make their own choices.

INTERPRETATION

What are we to make of all this? What conclusions should we draw from learning that chronic disease prevention policy in Cuba differs little from our own? The situation lends itself to several interpretations. First, it could vindicate the so-called victim-blaming disease prevention policies in the United States. Certainly this information makes it possible to claim, once more, that all any country can do in the face of chronic diseases is to beg people to change their habits. If Cuba, the socialist country that emphasizes health probably more than any nation in the world, construes health education as teaching individual responsibility for disease prevention, then it may be naive to criticize capitalist countries for doing the same thing. Such an interpretation could close the debate between progressives and mainstream health policy analysts and lead the critics to support the U.S. health promotion policies.

A second possible conclusion would use this information to dismiss Cuban policy as irrelevant. This interpretation would point out that all the concentration on Cuba implies, incorrectly, that that country is some kind of paragon. But many aspects of Cuban life are far from ideal. For example, sexism is rampant (despite the large numbers of women in high places); there is little freedom to express unorthodox political opinion (although literacy levels are very high for Latin America, all bright children are welcomed into higher education, and cultural self-expression is encouraged); and Cubans tend to treat social problems as though they were merely technical (a characteristic of societies that believe they have solved the basic political problems). Perhaps American analysts should just add chronic disease prevention policy to the list of Cuba's shortcomings, leave Cuba alone, and get on with the pressing disease prevention problems in our own country.

A third option would bring out the political nature of Cuba's health promotion policy. The policy is certainly not based solely on scientific information about its efficacy in reducing disease. One could argue that MINSAP, like the U.S. Department of Health and Human Services, emphasizes health promotion as a means of disease prevention because it does not threaten the economy. As I observed in chapter two, exercise, while great for a feeling of fitness, has a dubious relation to disease prevention. Many studies do show that exercise reduces the risk factors for heart attacks, but whether it reduces heart attacks themselves is not known.[34] Similarly, while smoking is clearly a major cause of both heart disease and cancer, the extent to which smoking alone causes illness is not entirely clear.[35] Cuba does have, as noted, a new occupational safety and health program, but so far MINSAP puts little emphasis on occupational toxins as a source of disease. And, with the important exception of pesticides, it has not yet devoted many resources to possible environmental threats to health.[36]

In addition, Cuban policy pays only minimal attention to the possible role of diet in disease causality. The Cuban diet is heavy on fried foods and sweets, practically devoid of fresh fruits and vegetables. The people, however, are still congratulating themselves on their success—certainly commendable, if not always perfect—in producing enough eggs, milk, meat, beans, and rice to feed generously the entire population. Questions about food tend to elicit answers that assume the issue is how to provide it. Few people talk about the possibility that chronic disease incidence might be lowered were Cuba drastically to reduce sugar production in order to grow and distribute locally many different kinds of food. Although the Cuban Institute of Nutrition conducts research into such questions, the concept that agriculture policy, food policy, and health might be linked is not part of the public discourse.

While any of these three possible conclusions would be worth developing, this chapter ends instead with a deeper look at a theme I have been pursuing all along: responsibility for health. Should disease prevention be an individual or a social responsibility? More to the point, what is the relationship between these two concepts? Let us look again at the criticism of health promotion policy in the United States discussed in chapter two. Basically there are two charges. First, the policy assumes, erroneously, that all Americans are equally able to change to healthy behavior. Second, the policy individualizes health, ignoring the social, economic, and political causes of behavior and of disease.

Are these charges applicable to Cuba? The first one probably is not, for Cuba really is a fairly egalitarian society. By no stretch of the imagination could one conclude that Cubans are all alike —in wealth, in education, or any other way. But no one is extremely poor, and no one is extremely rich. This state of affairs is enforced through such policies as the rationing of basic consumer goods, control on the sale and rent of housing, equal access to good medical care and education, and the elimination of unemployment. In other words, Cubans benefit pretty equally from economic production and thus have "lifestyles" that differ more according to differing personalities, talents, predispositions, and so on than according to differing economic resources. Especially this is so compared with capitalist countries. Therefore MINSAP can call on everyone to begin exercising and stop smoking with some confidence that people's economic capacities to do so are similar. This equality of ability to comply makes health promotion in Cuba more just than it is in the United States. So Cuban health promotion cannot be seriously criticized for ignoring social differences.

But health education there does seem to individualize health. It does call for personal rather than social change. To evaluate this policy, we need to ask what people mean when they say that the society—or the state, or the social structure—causes disease and is therefore responsible for its prevention. What, exactly, is "the society"? One possible answer emerged during my interview at a Havana policlinic. Near the end of a two-hour conversation with some half dozen policlinic staff members, I observed, "In the United States, our health education program is much like yours, but many people criticize it because it seems to make individuals culpable for their diseases." ("Blaming the victim," the psychologist interjected, in English. "Yes," I agreed.) "What do you think about that interpretation, that these methods individualize the problem?"

"Well, we begin with the basic assumption that the health of the people is a responsibility of the Cuban state. This is a very important point of departure. All the educative work is an element of support. It is the responsibility of the state to create healthy conditions of life. Education is a support."

This sounded to me consistent with Marxist principles but not a description of their chronic disease prevention policy, which relies almost entirely, it seems, on health education. Trying to clear up my confusion, I asked, "What does the state do then, to reduce, for example, cancer?" Several people spoke at once to answer. My tape recorder caught the following responses: "The state proposes. . . . It does research to demonstrate. . . . We have campaigns. . . . We demonstrate. . . ." Eventually one voice predominated. It was the physician's: "We have propaganda campaigns about the damage that cigarettes do. We give people enough information for them to be convinced. One of our primary systems is to let people arrive at their own understanding, where they themselves know that smoking is harmful. We don't do anything to try to force people not to smoke."

It remains unclear who the "we" is in these sentences. The doctor could have meant "we the state" or "we health educators." Certainly he blurred the distinction that had just been made between the state's responsibility to create healthy conditions of life and the responsibility of health education to support the state in this task. And so had the previous speakers. I had asked what the state does, and in answering, people referred to the state both as "it" and "we." Quite plausibly this meant that the policlinic staff members saw themselves as representatives of the state, just as, say, U.S. Department of Agriculture employees might refer to themselves as the state in a conversation on American agriculture policy. But whether the doctor was speaking for the state or for health educators, he was saying that what they do to prevent cancer is to try to get individuals to do something to prevent cancer. This formulation either gives the state no primary role in cancer prevention or obliterates the distinction between the individual and the state. And this seems to be precisely the point.

In socialist ideology the state *is* the individuals in it. Individuals create it and run it. And just as the family, in our minds, does not "exist" somehow separately from its members, so to many Cubans the socialist state has no separate reality apart from its citizens. At least this is the ideology. It differs so radically from liberal ideology's distinction between the individual and the society that Americans are likely to dismiss it. Claiming that Cubans take for granted a dialectical relation between the individual and the society sounds more like propaganda than description. And possibly it is. But the concept puts a whole new cast on evaluating Cuban chronic disease prevention policy. Certainly it helps explain the following remarks of the clinic's health educator as she picked up the comment about not forcing people to stop smoking:

> In addition, we can never say that someone who gets cancer of the lung is personally responsible because he smoked. It is a little bit our responsibility, too, for we haven't known how to help him sufficiently, how to help him stop smoking. Because when the group puts pressure on people, it produces changes. When the

group has a lot of knowledge about this situation and everyone becomes conscious of the problem, then group pressure is going to be most effective.

This switch to "the group" implies that by "we" she did not mean only "we health professionals." Rather, she seemed to mean the whole citizenry. She continued enthusiastically.

> It's the same with the habit of smoking. It's the same with obesity. Because now around my neighborhood we see everybody running together, everyone doing exercises together, riding bicycles together (finding one someplace or renting one).[37] So that this isn't a problem. Philosophically, we don't see things from the individual point of view. Philosophically we see things from the collective point of view because the collectivity influences, the collectivity pressures, and the collectivity is the best informed. The best knowledge is collective knowledge; it is going to influence everyone and, best of all, it is going to convince everyone. So it is not individual.

This is not the most lucid analysis one could hope for, but it does indicate a set of presuppositions about the relationship between the individual and the state that differ considerably from what my questions assumed. My questions had implied that individuals and the state are two conceptually distinct entities. The responses implied that "the state" is merely a way to refer to many individuals at once and that the term is interchangeable with "the collectivity," "the group," and "us."

American Marxists and other radicals sometimes interpret Marx's insistence that "social being" determines consciousness to mean that societies, not individuals, do things, or should do things. But such a formulation, relying as it does on abstractions, makes for grand generalizations and amorphous thinking. It reifies society and questions the efficacy and the morality of individual actions in the face of social problems. Most significantly, instead of offering a new way to consider the relation between the individual and the society, it merely accepts the old way—seeing these two things as opposites—and reverses the emphasis.

The "new way" to consider the relation between the individual and the society proposes that human beings only exist and have consciousness of themselves within societies. It is not just that individuals create societies, but that societies create individuals. Each includes the other. This concept, Shlomo Avineri points out, "makes quite irrelevant the question whether change in individuals will precede change in circumstances or vice versa. As 'society' does not exist . . . as an entity distinct from 'individuals', change in individuals is *ipso facto* also change in society, for change in social circumstances is also change in individuals."[38]

If "society" does not exist, the idea that the "state" has an existence apart from individuals is at least equally, perhaps more, problematic. And if the state can most accurately be conceptualized as a collection of individuals, then one cannot logically separate the state's responsibility for disease prevention from the individual's responsibility. To do so would be like calling on the family to engage in some collective activity—to clean up the house, for example—and then saying that none of the members of the family had to participate. This is an especially apt analogy because a major thing that Cubans are expected to do is participate. Participation is at the heart of the revolution. It can be seen as Cuba's practice of the theory that the state and the individual create one another.

Health was an early application. Right after the revolution, for example, the CDRs took up the problem of neighborhood sanitation. To reduce infectious and parasitic diseases, they called on everyone in the neighborhood to clean up garbage around their houses; to get rid of mosquito breeding sites in their yards, patios, and balconies; to boil water before drinking; to wear shoes; and to get inoculations. The campaign is given credit for much of the reduction in morbidity and mortality that occurred in the early 1960s. Were these actions individual or social? Clearly, individual people did them, but just as clearly, even if "the society" had done them, the actual work would have been done by individual men and women. Does it matter whether the person who cleans up the neighborhood is hired by the government and paid a salary to do so, or whether that person, voluntarily, along with his or her neighbors, does so? The critics of mainstream health education apparently believe that a disease prevention policy that assigns such tasks to individuals is unjust. But the Cubans I spoke with seemed to be saying that in a truly socialist country, such work *should* be done by individual volunteers and that rather than blaming the victim, the policy both reflects and advances the consciousness that the society is responsible for health and that "we" constitute the society. In other words, what U.S. critics call "individual responsibility," Cubans—at least those who support the government—see as individual participation.

One final note, I do not mean to gloss over the question of power. If Cubans have more and more responsibility (and the establishment in 1977 of a sort of people's legislative branch of government—Poder Popular—suggests that they do)[39] but not more power, then the new consciousness is a sham. The empirical question of where the political power actually lies in Cuba has not been forthrightly addressed by enthusiasts for the regime, either inside or outside Cuba. But my point is more normative. Can a nation's health policy ever justly give individuals responsibility for disease prevention? The answer proposed here is a qualified yes. It can if it equally distributes goods and services —and power—so that the conceptual distinction between individuals and society dissolves. Whether any nation, including Cuba, actually does this is another question.

CHAPTER 5

Air Traffic Control
and Stress

J ust as the assumption of a simple dichotomy between the individual and society influences our ideas about disease prevention, so do other dualisms. This chapter concerns the belief that objective and subjective phenomena can be clearly distinguished. The case in point is the study of stress. In the last decade an explosion of scientific and popular books and articles has promoted the hypothesis that stress causes disease. Examining a wide variety of pathologies—from coronary heart disease and stroke, through peptic ulcers, diabetes, and skin diseases, to tumors—the literature proposes, with varying degrees of certitude, that a major etiology is stress. This hypothesis marks a radical departure from the disease causality theory that has dominated medicine for the last hundred years: it suggests that diseases can occur without noxious physical substances. The stress theory offers no bacteria or viruses, no parasites, no chemicals, no toxins or poisons. Instead, it posits social events as the cause of diseases. The stress theory is thus of great interest to those who argue that an effective understanding of disease demands an investigation of the political and economic settings in which disease occurs. Because the stress theory advances no tangible substance as the cause of disease, the only etiologic phenomena one *can* investigate are social or emotional. The enthusiasm this realization has induced among social epidemiologists resembles that engendered by the germ theory in the late nineteenth century. Like the germ theory before it, the stress theory promises to apply to nearly all illnesses. Indeed it transcends ordinary illness, some people argue, for stress may be a basic cause of all pathology, not only physical disease, but mental disorders and social deviance as well. The stress theory invites sociologists, psychologists, anthropologists, economists, and political scientists into the medical discourse, newly legitimizing social science's persistent attempts to draw attention to the nonmedical components of disease.

Among the proponents of the stress theory, occupational safety and health professionals stand out because their research has the clearest public policy implications. It can help or hinder change in the job conditions encountered by millions of working men and women. The notion that intangible conditions on the job can cause chronic diseases and exacerbate infectious ones has been heavily promoted in the last few years by the safety and health committees of many labor unions and by community-based labor organizations such as the Committees on Occupational Safety and Health (COSH groups). These committees and groups were first formed, in most cases, after the passage of the 1970 Occupational Safety and Health Act in order to alert workers to their new right to be protected against toxic fibers, gasses, fumes, solvents, and other industrial hazards. With the development of the stress theory, however, health and safety groups began to extend their interest beyond hazardous substances to include the social conditions on the job as well. No longer restricted to a concern about toxic matter in their quest for occupational safety and health, they could justifiably encompass every negative aspect of work, including job insecurity, sexual harassment, low pay, racism, conflicting demands, forced overtime, and lack of recognition, control, or respect. The stress theory of disease causality provided a scientific rationale for labor unions and for COSH groups to argue not only for a clean workplace but also for a just and democratic one. It transformed the issue of social relations on the job from the subjective, moral realm to the objective, scientific one. Not surprisingly, it has proved an effective tool to strengthen unions. Unfortunately, it may backfire.

Despite the compelling nature of the stress theory, the attempt to investigate the relation between trying social events and disease poses important empirical and normative dilemmas. Central among them is whether such investigations inappropriately scientize social phenomena. While social events such as job conditions most probably do have some causal relation to disease, studying that proposition scientifically necessarily reduces and may thereby distort the phenomena under investigation. As a whole generation of philosophers and social scientists have reasoned, science, a method developed to investigate and describe empirical reality, possesses only limited ability to apprehend the social world.[1] Thus it inevitably fails to capture much of the kaleidoscopic array of interacting experiences, emotions, and values generally subsumed under the word *stress*. Further, it may exacerbate the very conditions people experience as stressful, for the stress theory requires the services of experts. Consequently it takes from workers, who already may be suffering from loss of control over their jobs, the ability even to describe authoritatively the conditions under which they work. In addition, the theory makes health the primary criterion on which to base the abolition of intolerable conditions. Whereas workers should be able to point to a degrading or exhausting job and to argue, invoking principles of human dignity, that no one should have to live that way, the scientization of stress makes it difficult to censure a job if that job does not have negative health consequences. Given the fact that no scientific studies have yet reported a clear causal relation between particular social experiences and disease in humans,[2] the stress theory, ironically, can easily be used to bolster the arguments of those who object to changing the status quo. Thus, while the stress theory of disease causality puts forward a promising alternative to the narrow biologic model of health and disease, it may at the same time utilize science to legitimize a perpetuation of objectionable social conditions.

In this chapter I discuss that paradox, using as an example the phenomenon of stress in air traffic control as it was expressed at the time of the Professional Air Traffic Controllers Organization (PATCO) strike against the U.S. Federal Aviation Administration (FAA) in 1981. An examination of the congressional hearings before and after the strike shows that workers may not find it in their interests to use the words *stress* or *stressful* when appealing for better job conditions or more benefits. Instead, they may be better off describing their jobs in terminology that keeps the issue outside the scientific arena.

AIR TRAFFIC CONTROLLERS STRIKE

Air traffic controllers have long complained about their jobs. In 1968, just after PATCO was created, controllers staged a series of work slowdowns in protest against the demands and pressures of their work. The slowdowns were eventually halted in 1969, but in 1980 relations between PATCO and the FAA were again so acrimonious that controllers began to talk about calling a strike. In early January of 1981, PATCO, nearing the end of its contract with the FAA, submitted a new contract proposing major changes in controller benefits. The proposal's most controversial features were an across-the-board $10,000 increase in pay, plus various kinds of overtime and cost-of-living increases that would have made basic controller pay range between $22,266 and $73,470 a year and given some controllers over $100,000 annually. In addition, PATCO asked for a four-day work week and generous new (and earlier) retirement benefits. Negotiations began in early February 1981 and proceeded slowly. The old contract expired in mid-March and, although talks between the FAA and PATCO continued, they went badly. At the end of May, the controllers threatened to walk out on 22 June. Four days before the deadline, a congressional subcommittee called a hearing in hopes of forestalling the strike. Those two days of testimony led to a marathon session between the FAA and PATCO during which leaders of the two groups finally agreed on a contract and the strike seemed to be averted. But PATCO's fifteen thousand members overwhelmingly rejected the agreement, and on 3 August 1981, 80 percent of them walked off their jobs, declaring a nationwide strike against FAA. In retaliation, the Reagan Administration fired the striking controllers and dissolved the union.

It was not a popular strike. Most Americans agreed with the administration that the PATCO strike was illegal and that the new salary and benefit demands were excessive. Even those Americans comprising the political left, that loose structure of progressives which might have been counted on to mount boycotts or in some other fashion support the strikers, failed to rally around PATCO. With some exceptions,[3] the left, partly motivated by the knowledge that PATCO had backed Ronald Reagan in the 1980 presidential campaign, ignored this labor dispute. Journalists who did support the strike generalized it, emphasizing the effects of Reagan's action on the labor movement as a whole.

This lack of vigorous support by leftists may also have derived from current thinking among progressive occupational health and safety analysts about political tactics. Left-leaning professionals concerned with job conditions have in recent years developed strong positions against industry's traditional assertion that compensation is the appropriate response to job hazards and that most occupational accidents and illnesses are caused by worker carelessness. Compensation, they argue, is fundamentally unjust. Instead, the goal should be the elimination of the hazards themselves. Similarly, they reason that safety and health result from the structure of the workplace, not from the behavior of individual workers.[4] This thinking, developed around physical and chemical hazards, has come to include the more abstract hazard of job stress.[5] From the progressive point of view, the knowledge that a job is stressful should lead to the conclusion that many of its basic characteristics should be changed or at least ameliorated. The air traffic controllers, however, evinced little interest in an anticompensation view. They did not want change; they wanted money. They were clear about wanting less *exposure* to job conditions—in other words, they wanted less time at work—but they did not suggest any basic alteration of those conditions.[6] In that respect, then, the controllers and their employers were not far apart as negotiations began. Neither side was interested in substantial changes in job conditions.

In regard to whether the stress problem was an individual one, however, the two groups were in fundamental conflict. The conflict was reflected dramatically in their separate understanding of what "stress" means. Characterizing all their exchanges—at least in congressional hearings, and there is no reason to doubt that this was also true during contract negotiations—was a disagreement over the definition of stress. The disagreement was never formally acknowledged, and the confusion that resulted not only inhibited clear communication but, the record makes clear, aided the FAA's eventual triumph over PATCO. Although members and supporters of both groups occasionally used such garbled language that it was hard to tell *what* they meant by stress, for the most part, people taking a procontroller position described stress as synonymous with the job conditions themselves, particularly the pressure, tension, strain, and demands. In contrast, people representing or supporting the FAA either presented stress purely as a reaction to those conditions or devoted all their attention to the variety of physical and psychological responses to those stressful jobs. Thus, while most controllers thought of stress as one of the inherent characteristics of guiding aircraft, their employers tended to regard it as an individual phenomenon experienced only by some workers.

Trying to dramatize their position, some controllers claimed that job conditions, in addition to being the essence of stress, also cause physical, emotional, and social problems. Their argument about causal links was, however, usually different from the FAA's. Controllers seemed to mean, "Not only is air traffic control inherently stressful, but it *also* has negative consequences." The FAA argument, on the other hand, consistently made causality primary. Only the verifiable consequences of air traffic control were of concern. FAA spokespersons avoided discussing the proposal that controlling air traffic is inherently tense, demanding, anxiety producing—or "stressful." Such different conceptualizations of the fundamental issue made communication between the two groups a matter of parallel discussions. They usually talked past, not to, one another.

1979 TESTIMONY

These differing assumptions about stress were first illustrated in congressional hearings in the summer of 1979 called to consider testimony on four bills introduced into the House of Representatives that would extend to other controllers the benefits enjoyed by Department of Transportation controllers. In her opening remarks, subcommittee chairwoman Rep. Patricia Schroeder directed attention to stress. She took a procontroller position by implicitly defining stress as the job conditions themselves. In addition, she listed some presumed consequences of those conditions:

> This is an exacting and precise job, leaving little time for contemplation and tolerating no error whatsoever. It seems to me that the stress of the occupation is self evident. This stress can result in early leaving of the services, personal problems, and disorders, both physical and psychological. If we, as a society, ask these men and women to perform this essential but ultimately debilitating function, we, as a society, must be responsible for the future welfare of the workers.[7]

Jerry Byrd, a military controller from Alabama, also defined stress as the job itself:

> I speak as one who has personally experienced the mental and physical strain of controlling aircraft in and out of busy airports; as one who has experienced the stress of staying on the radar scope or in the tower for long periods of time without a break; as one who has been confronted with the necessity of making successive decisions carrying life and death consequences—where the standard is always perfection. . . .
>
> I also speak as one who has seen the controllers break down and weep, on the job, as the result of the intense pressure and

constant demand to speed the flow of traffic—knowing full well that the impending rush of air traffic will exceed his reasonable capacity, but also knowing that he must operate at the limits of his capabilities, on the brink of human disaster, for as long as necessary.[8]

In contrast to these and other experiential reports, Charles Weithoner, an associate administrator of the FAA, submitted testimony that defined stress in biochemical terms:

> Over the past ten years, scientists from the FAA Civil Aeromedical Institute have conducted physiological, biochemical and psychological measurement on air traffic specialists . . . in an attempt to provide a general characterization of the stress of air traffic control work. . . . Heart rates were recorded . . . excretion of three stress-related hormones was measured . . . [and] using psychological questionnaires, tendency to experience anxiety was assessed.[9]

Weithoner ended a brief synopsis of these studies by stating:

> In conclusion, this extensive research supports the view that it is inappropriate to describe air traffic control work, as is commonly done in the popular press, as an unusually stressful occupation.[10]

Picking out a particular FAA study to emphasize this conclusion, Weithoner reported on research on thirteen controllers in Oklahoma City:

> Heart rate and hormone excretion data indicated that work at these facilities produced a relatively low degree of stress. Although these personnel reported a relatively higher but entirely normal tendency to experience anxiety than the center and tower specialists that have been studied, their duty-related arousal was similar to that measured in low-density centers and towers.
>
> This study, even though conducted on small numbers of personnel within distinct geographical limits, produces the same conclusion as that reached with respect to all other air traffic control work: flight service station work is not an unusually stressful occupation.[11]

This is a substantially different kind of testimony. Not only does it assume to report on things as they objectively *are* in contrast to things as they subjectively *seem*, but it draws on a different understanding of stress. Representative Schroeder defined stress as an exacting and precise job that leaves no time for contemplation and tolerates no error. Similarly, Byrd defined stress as staying at a radar scope for long periods, making crucial decisions under intense demand and constant pressure. Weithoner, however, defined stress as increased heart rate and hormone production. By measuring those variables, he claimed to demonstrate that the previous testimony was in error. In essence he said, "We measured stress and found that the controllers have very little." Then he relabeled what the controllers had called stress and dubbed it "anxiety." This other thing—anxiety—is indeed present, he testified, but that is "entirely normal." It is not an issue.

This conversion of the word *stress* from a term that refers to the overall experience of guiding aircraft to one referring to the body's biochemical reaction to that experience fundamentally changes the debate. It shifts the focus from the conditions under which air traffic controllers work to the people who do the work. It makes workers, not the job, the locus of the problem. It also presupposes that the major concern is causality. It is not, however, erroneous in any sense. Since the late 1930s a growing body of literature has carefully detailed the regular physiological responses of the human body to what are essentially social events and has called the responses "stress."

DEFINITIONS OF STRESS

Hans Selye, the father of stress research, first employed the word *stress* in the late 1930s to refer to "a stereotyped pattern of biochemical, functional and structural changes" within the body in response to "increased demand."[12] He distinguished *stress*, a bodily condition, from *stressor*, the agent of that condition.[13] He also pointed out that the body does not discriminate between pleasant and unpleasant demands or stressors: "All that counts is the intensity of the demand for readjustment or adaptation. . . . It is difficult to see at first how such essentially different things as cold, heat, drugs, hormones, sorrow, and joy could provoke an identical biologic reaction. Nevertheless, this is the case."[14] Selye argued that stress is biologic in nature, noting that the characteristic response can occur even during anesthesia. Stress, he said, is "thus not identical to emotional arousal or nervous tension." Nor is stress something to be avoided: "Indeed it cannot be avoided, since just staying alive creates some demand for life-maintaining energy." In addition, because stress is nonspecific and occurs with a variety of stimuli, there can be no particular stress. Such terms as "emotional stress, surgical stress, flying stress . . . cold stress . . . social stress, and so on" are misleading, he insisted. Stress is thus a normal biologic function. It is a regular adaptation to everyday life, of interest to medicine only when the hormonal changes, persisting abnormally, may be a precursor to illness.[15]

This definition of stress, however, is only one of at least three others. Regardless of Selye's claim that stress is not identical to emotional arousal, the layperson today usually thinks of stress as an emotion. In ordinary language, stress is similar to tension, anxiety, or pressure. This common understanding has been advanced by a number of psychologists who propose a typology of personalities. They suggest that men and women can be divided into "type A" and "type B" personalities.[16] Their hypothesis is that some people—those C. L. Cooper calls "stressful people"[17] —usually feel impatient, driven, and competitive and are more prone to coronary heart disease than are more relaxed men and women.

A third meaning for stress is employed by a number of sociologists who, also ignoring Selye's terminology, have given the name "stress" to that which Selye called "stressors." For example: "For the purposes of this presentation, stress will be regarded as a force or stimulus, whatever its form may be, which provokes the organism to respond in a condition of disturbance";[18] and "In this report 'stress' refers to any characteristic of the *environment* which poses a threat to the individual."[19] Research on the environment or stimulus included in this definition falls into two main research areas. One concerns itself with the connection between disease and unusual "life events."[20] The other focuses on "occupational stress," that is, the routine aspects of jobs that place heavy demands on people.[21]

In yet a fourth usage, stress is disease itself. "Stress," says Stanley Aronowitz, "has become the black lung of the technical class."[22] Similarly, Joseph Eyer and Peter Sterling remark that "the group entering the labor market between 1880 and 1925 experienced a larger upswing of pathology, starting from lower levels. Of the many factors contributing to this rise in stress at the turn of the century, the alienation and intensification of work was perhaps the most important."[23] And: "That knot in your stomach, the stiffness in your neck, the ache in your temples, are just what you think—stress."[24]

It is important to point out that no one can claim to use the "real" definition of stress. The word stands for a concept, not a thing. It is more like the terms *power* or *IQ* than like *book* or *cloud*, and therefore means whatever anyone says it means.[25] It is also noteworthy that despite the sharply different definitions for stress, people are rarely confused about its meaning in general conversation. Indeed, not uncommonly scientists use more than one definition in the same article, without, apparently, failing to communicate.[26] So, the fact that stress means many things would not matter except for one hindrance. In arguments between labor and management, as we have seen, the biologic definition can be used to refute testimony employing the sociological definition, without anyone calling attention to the fact that management and labor, using the same word, each refer to a different thing.

To recapitulate, the air traffic controllers used stress primarily in the sociological sense. Although they occasionally made use of the psychological or biologic definitions, for them, stress mainly meant demanding job conditions. This definition places the problem in the social environment. The FAA, in contrast, while sometimes giving stress a sociological meaning, emphasized the psychological and biochemical definitions. Thus, it placed the problem inside people. Unfortunately for their case, the controllers frequently claimed that the stress in their jobs causes physical and mental pathology. They therefore allowed into the debate physiologists and psychologists who, because they individualized stress, could legitimately argue that reducing stress means changing people, not necessarily changing the conditions in which they work.

1981 TESTIMONY

In 1981 another congressional hearing displayed the unacknowledged, unrecognized struggle over the definition of stress. That April, a House subcommittee called for testimony to determine why the contract negotiations between the FAA and PATCO were breaking down. Like the hearing two years earlier, this one contained statements from PATCO spokespeople and some of their supporters in Congress implicitly maintaining that stress refers to the tensions inherent in air traffic control. It also contained testimony from the FAA and its supporters that concentrated on the human body.

PATCO President Robert Poli spoke early in the hearing, urging Congress to consider the conditions under which controllers work:

> Controllers constantly face countless situations which require them to make decisions affecting the lives of thousands of people. . . . Day in and day out, they must guard against even the smallest error, for a mistake could kill hundreds. There is no room for guesswork, nor is there time to sit back and leisurely consider a traffic situation. Decisions must be swift, positive, and correct. . . . Controllers must learn to live under extraordinary pressure that never really goes away.[27]

Instead of leaving it at that, however, he went on to tie these job conditions to their presumed consequences:

Over time, while dreading the terrible consequences of one incorrect control decision, the controller loses the fight to the knowledge that he is human and, in the long run, fallible. The strain created by this internal war generates insidious effects on the controller's entire life. They can manifest themselves in physical or mental disorders, social withdrawal, marital trouble or concealed alcoholism.[28]

Poli then asserted that 89 percent of controllers are forced to retire early "because an FAA flight surgeon has found that their health has deteriorated to the point that they cannot be allowed to continue."[29]

Following up on this claim about the consequences of air traffic control, Subcommittee Chairperson Mary Rose Oakar asked if the controllers had "medical studies . . . which indicate the effect of stress on the general health and well being of air traffic controllers."[30] Poli responded somewhat uneasily:

> Yes, we do. There has been a study done by Dr. Rose of Boston University. Controversial study, to say the least. It is interesting to me that the FAA uses parts of that study when they want to say bad things about controllers. But the parts of the study which speak to hypertension or speak to the difficulty of being an air traffic controller or speak to the difficulty which exists in an employment relationship with the FAA and air traffic controllers . . . those do not seem to come up from the FAA. But we certainly will submit a copy of that study to your subcommittee.[31]

Poli had reason to be uneasy, for the report in question,[32] the most extensive study of air traffic controllers to date, employs definitions of stress and uses a methodology that serve the interests of the FAA more than those of the controllers. In addition, it gives only moderate support to the hypothesis that the job has negative consequences. Clifton von Kann, president of the National Aeronautic Association, a professional organization that identifies with the FAA, made effective use of the Rose report in the testimony he prepared for the April hearing:

> The union has claimed that controlling air traffic has a bad effect on health. This is not borne out by the five-year health change

study conducted by Dr. Robert Rose of the Boston University Medical School. . . . In brief the report suggests that there are no medical problems with controllers that are not found in any occupation. More importantly the study strongly indicates that the solution lies in a better selection process and better management-labor practices—not in paying controllers Vice Presidential salaries.[33]

Von Kann concluded:

Although PATCO has placed a significant emphasis on mental and physical health deterioration because of the nature of air traffic control work, no studies have confirmed that the control of air traffic is uniquely hazardous to an employee's health when compared to other demanding vocations. With respect to the length of career or the effects of stress, no studies have confirmed that controllers cannot function efficiently throughout a normal career or that stress depreciates either health or performance.[34]

With the possible exception of references to the comparative seriousness of the controllers' medical problems, these statements accurately reflect the conclusions of this study.

ROSE REPORT

The Rose study, undertaken in 1973 with a $2.8 million contract from the FAA, was prompted by an earlier FAA report which, according to Rose et al., "suggested that the FAA needed to document not only the degree of job stress in air traffic control work, but also the impact this stress might have on the physical and psychological health of the controllers."[35] The new study's major finding was that controllers have 50–100 percent more hypertension than other American men their ages.[36] Rose and his associates were reluctant, however, to attribute that hypertension to the job of controlling air traffic: "We did not find the ATC work environment and the workload within that environment were the most predictive factors for illness. Rather, we found that particular types of people with their own personal, psychological, and biological reactions were susceptible to illness when placed in the air traffic control environment."[37]

This statement raises questions about definitions. It is significant that nowhere in the massive (655 pages of text plus 160 pages of appendixes) report do Rose and his colleagues explicitly define stress. When they use the term they give it one of two different meanings. First, they imply that stress is the job or something about the job. In partial response to one of the FAA's specific questions, "Do controllers experience stress?" they said, "Interestingly, those ATCs who *responded to difficult days on the job* with low cortisol or low variability in blood pressure were more prone to have mild or moderate illnesses during the course of the study. We think that there was a suppression of their physiological system, and this may have represented their way of *responding to stress*."[38] The authors also imply that stress is the job or something about the job in the following statement: "For this study we hypothesized that *stress would be reflected* in the differences in blood pressure, in cortisol and growth hormones and in behavior among and within men while working under conditions of varying difficulties."[39] And, later in the conclusion, they note approvingly that a previous FAA study defined stress as "any characteristics of the job environment which pose a threat to the individual."[40]

The Rose study also implies, however, that the word *stress* refers to *reactions* to the job, sometimes seeming to define it as emotions, other times as biochemical secretions. Controllers, they write, "differ in their experience of stress . . . but its sources are not determinable."[41] They further claim, "The stress level, we believe, is not altogether dependent on the occupational activity and hazards, but is determined in part by the psychological and physiological 'interpreters' of the individual."[42]

Confusion about the definition of stress notwithstanding, Rose and his colleagues set out to test the assumption that job stress causes disease. They treat it as a hypothesis. In other words, they posit the job as analogous to a chemical or virus suspected of being toxic and make it their task to learn whether the job indeed threatens health or whether it is benign. This approach fundamentally misconceives the issue, for while chemicals and viruses are physical substances, both "difficult days on the job" and "stress" (when it is construed as difficult days on the job) are abstractions. If careful research proves a suspect chemical nontoxic, people know they can work safely with it. But if research shows that a demanding and difficult job does not cause disease, the job nevertheless remains demanding and difficult. To put it another way, "toxic chemical" and "stressful job" are conceptually dissimilar categories. It is possible to describe a chemical separately from its toxic properties, but the description of a job—what people do at work—includes those things about it that are stressful. Without its stressful elements, a job changes its specific characteristics. If not toxic, however, a chemical remains exactly the same chemical.

But "jobs" and "chemicals" have an important characteristic in common that the Rose report also fails to recognize: neither retains its essence if it is broken down into its parts. Benzene, for example, entirely vanishes when it is broken down into the six molecules of carbon and the six molecules of hydrogen of which it is composed. Similarly, the job of air traffic control tends to disappear when divided into components. Workers, as the controllers keep insisting, view their jobs as integrating objective phenomena and subjective experiences. They do not experience the activity of the job separately from the environment in which they perform the activity. For them, the job by definition includes observable physical actions as well as nonempirical subjectivities such as attitudes about these actions, relations both among the people doing them and between those workers and their supervisors, and the significance the actions have. Unless all these features appear together, there is no meaningful way that the "job" exists.

Strange as it seems, Rose and his colleagues never attempted to describe the controller's job. Instead, they identified certain quantifiable physical and emotional components of air traffic control, assuming both that what they identified encompassed the job and that the job was merely the sum of its parts. Although they employed various terms for the components throughout the report, the features they most consistently referred to are: (1) work activity (a category that includes workload); (2) context (used interchangeably with work environment); and (3) attitudes and feelings (including degree of satisfaction, investment, and alienation). Such a division lends itself to bias. Because the categories are arbitrary and the relations among them vague (for example, why are attitudes and feelings a separate category from the context of work?), researchers can concentrate on some components and give others short shrift. And this is precisely what happened. The Rose report concentrates on the individual psychological reaction of the controllers to their work. Despite their description of the study as one laying to rest "years of controversy over alleged difficulties and effects of the work on the health of controllers,"[43] the separation of the job into discrete entities reveals that Rose et al. are less interested in the effects of the work than they are in differences among the workers. They note that "recent researchers have selected and rigorously pursued certain areas of investigation which may be crucial in determining the extent to which social and psychological factors influence health." But instead of talking about social factors, the authors go on to list individual and psychological ones: "Included among these crucial areas are individual differences in hormonal and cardiovascular responses to stressful stimuli, the impact of life events, individual differences in ability to adapt to changes in environmental demands, and individual differences in behavioral life styles. . . . Given reliable methodology and evidence of their relevance to health change, these areas served to focus our selection of variables for this study."[44]

The point is not that individual psychological reactions are insignificant. Jobs, as people experience them, do include psychological factors. The point is that to *concentrate* on personal responses is ideological. Such a concentration, unconsciously reflecting the dominant beliefs about the social order, assumes without justification or explanation that the individual is the basic unit. This ideological assumption is not peculiar to the Rose study, for it informs most studies of stress and is their major contradiction. Stress research, promising to enlarge our understanding of disease causality by including social factors, inevitably defines those social factors so narrowly, reducing them to individual psychological differences, that it merely reproduces the inveterate germ theory it set out to augment. As Allan Young points out, it desocializes the social determinants of illness.[45]

The emphasis on the individual serves the interests of management in exonerating itself from responsibility for health changes among employees. For example, after saying that the controllers who became ill during the study were those who, although competent, perceived their work negatively, were dissatisfied with it, felt alienated from it, and drank too much, Rose and his colleagues concluded: "These findings suggest that it was not so much what they were doing but the context in which they were doing it and the attitudes and feelings they had about their situation that influenced their risk for health change."[46] This, of course, echoes the finding quoted earlier, that the "work environment and the workload" were less predictive of illness than were "particular types of people with their own personal, psychological, and biological reactions."[47] It also restates the conclusion that "the stress level . . . is not altogether dependent on occupational activities and hazards but is determined in part by the psychological and physiological 'interpreters' of the individual."[48]

There is not a little irony in a major study on stress coming to this conclusion. The whole point of the stress theory is that the body reacts physiologically to the social and psychological environment. Selye's work deserves its fame precisely because it proves the ancient Hippocratic dictum that the mind and body are interdependent, not separately operating entities. The stress theory thus challenges an assumption central to the medical practice that developed with the germ theory: that every disease has a specific etiology. It dictates instead that disease results from a host of interactions among physical and social phenomena and the meaning or interpretations people give to them. The stress theory *adds* psychology and emotions to disease causality; it does not separate them out.

Rose and his colleagues misconstrued the theory. They gave it a distorting twist by conceptually divorcing work from the way people interpret work, separating the work environment from the attitudes and feelings of people in the environment, disconnecting what people do from the context in which they do it. In other words, they unwittingly brought to a study of the diseases most obviously caused by the interacting social, physical, and emotional environment, those tools of analysis developed specifically to disaggregate the physical from the social and the social from the emotional. The result was to place responsibility on—to blame—controllers for their illnesses.

The controllers also misconceived the issue. It *is* important to uncover correlations between jobs and disease. To be able to demonstrate that terrible job conditions can cause or exacerbate illness advances our understanding of disease causality. Terrible job conditions are, however, undesirable regardless of their ability to cause disease. Even if people could work at them in perfect health, they should, in a just society, be changed. The air traffic controllers' error was to insist that health was the major problem and that stress was the culprit. In doing so, they turned over to science, along with responsibility for showing the link between the job and disease, the capacity to identify those parts of the job that are undesirable. But only the people who work at jobs day after day really know what about them is demanding, tense, and unpleasant. Outsiders can merely guess, at best. And here is the crux of it: If the unpleasant aspects of the job are precisely those aspects that make it unhealthy, then to make a job both more pleasant and more healthy, one need simply ask the people who do it what they find intolerable. Why go through all the convoluted techniques of behavioral science in order to re-present in scientific terms the feelings and attitudes workers readily express? Why not just listen to them describe the things they want changed and then see about changing them?

The scientization of job conditions not only robs workers of control over the description of their jobs but can lend itself to severe distortions of that description. More to the point, to equate undesirable job conditions with the plastic term *stress* can sanction making workers themselves the fundamental problem. The final congressional hearing provides a striking example of such distortion.

POSTSTRIKE TESTIMONY

A month after the walkout, the National Transportation Safety Board (NTSB), an independent agency of the U.S. Department of Transportation, undertook an investigation into the safety of air transport. In this report the NTSB, exploiting the ambiguity of the word *stress*, introduced a new concept: stress and fatigue.[49] No longer was stress a singular term; it was, throughout the report, teamed up with fatigue. The Safety Board's principal conclusion after interviewing the new controllers and their supervisors was that the poststrike work force was not experiencing undue "stress and fatigue." The board was, however, "concerned that the long-term effect of the current work schedules will lead to fatigue and stress, which may eventually degrade controller efficiency and aviation safety."[50] The board recommended that the FAA devise a program "to detect the onset of, and to alleviate, controller fatigue and stress."[51]

When questioned about the findings of this study, James King, the chairman of the NTSB, did not explain to the congressional subcommittee why the report linked stress to fatigue in this way. He did say that fatigue "can be one of the symptoms" of stress,[52] but he also recited a list of other symptoms: "Well, there are some clinical symptoms in stress and fatigue, change or disruption of sleep and weight patterns, increase in nervous habits, increased smoking or alcohol use, increased impatience, change in eating patterns, gain or loss of weight, decreased sociability, and decreased tolerance to things such as noise. Lethargy. Those are some of the examples of the kinds of things that serve as indicators."[53] Whatever the reason, making stress virtually synonymous with fatigue diminishes stress. By calling it variously "stress/fatigue" and "stress and fatigue," the report suggested that the complex synthesis of intensity, fear, responsibility, and competence that the controllers described was something ordinary and mundane, something regularly experienced by everyone, something naturally part of every job.

More important, however, making stress similar to fatigue helped the FAA to turn stress into precisely the reverse of what the union had sought to describe. At the end of this final hearing on the PATCO walkout, the FAA administrator, J. Lynn Helms, responded to the NTSB investigation. In a letter to King later submitted to the subcommittee, he first drew upon the Rose report to support his contention that stress, instead of being synonymous with the job of air traffic control, or at least with difficult days, may not exist at all. He termed it "perceived stress." In addition, he alluded to the Rose report's argument that before the PATCO strike the most significant "attitudes and feelings" among controllers were alienation and divisiveness and that responsibility for them lay with PATCO.[54] The Rose report, he wrote, "clearly indicated that workload and the work itself were not the sources of health change effects or perceived stress. Rather, it was the context or environment within which the work was performed that was the major source of perceived stress. The clear inference from the report is that the adversary relationship that existed between management and the controllers' union created an atmosphere conducive to the developing of perceived stress."[55] Then Helms picked up the NTSB notion that stress is the same as fatigue and suggested that only some controllers "get" it: "The FAA has . . . initiated a review to consider the need for, and method of, conducting a monitoring system which would serve to identify controllers who might be suffering from fatigue and stress."[56]

In congressional testimony Helms took that interpretation one step farther. He converted stress into the PATCO members themselves. How, he was asked, does the FAA expect to avoid the strained employee–management relations that characterized the prestrike condition? He answered: refrain from rehiring PATCO members. "This stack of letters was written to me by FAA employees on one subject: don't bring these controllers back, it will be stress and fatigue."[57] "Our people tell us," he continued, "that fatigue walked out and now they are having fun like it was 15 to 20 years ago."[58]

LIMITS TO SCIENCE

Union organizers, rank-and-file members, and community occupational health and safety activists have in recent years eagerly adopted the language of stress. Once-dispirited workers, especially, embrace the stress thesis, for it can legitimize long-held complaints about job conditions, giving people a powerful theory with which to organize their knowledge about the circumstances of work. Instead of talking about shift work, speedups, or overbearing supervisors, they can talk about stress, a scientific concept that dignifies their grievances. The concept admits them into a community formerly inhabited only by executives. This ability to draw on the prestigious concepts of science to justify their appeals for change gives workers new hope for the future and promises to invigorate the whole union movement. But the faith that science will be effective where politics has failed seriously overestimates science and misunderstands its inherent biases. The PATCO case illustrates three arguments against using the stress discourse.

First, clinging to the stress theory gives those who control job conditions a new reason to ignore workers' complaints unless their jobs can convincingly be correlated with physical illness. Employing the stress theory narrows the claims that workers can make about their jobs, channeling everything into a circumscribed medical discourse and potentially limiting the sorts of onerous job conditions needing redress. At the same time, because only weak data support the stress hypothesis, claims for changes at the workplace based on it are subject to continual challenge. Consider the difference between arguing that a condition must be changed because everyone hates it and arguing that the condition must be changed because it is stressful. In the former, there are no rational grounds for a counterargument that the condition is benign; in the latter, anyone so inclined can confuse the issue by asking for objective evidence of the condition's stressful nature. Furthermore, it is possible to raise endless objections to the methodology of stress research, just as in any occupational health research. Thus the introduction of the stress theory into the labor-management dialogue may supply a new justification for delaying needed improvements in working conditions.

A second argument is that the stress discourse invalidates the experiences of ordinary people. It translates what people say about their jobs—eloquent and moving descriptions, many of them—into a technical language meaningless except to a small band of elite scientists and policy makers. Such a translation shuts ordinary people out of decision making that crucially affects their lives, turning their tensions and anxieties into a subject fit only for experts. At the same time, it elevates the possessors of the technical language, exacerbating the division among classes and weakening egalitarianism.

Many social critics cite the lack of community as a major problem in contemporary industrial society. Cut off from one another by the ethic of competition, Americans are said to seek few close relations and to be tuned instead to gaining and maintaining places for themselves in the social hierarchy. Stress research exacerbates the tendency to form hierarchies, for it places one more phenomenon—the intuitive, experiential knowledge people have about their work—in the realm of professionals, sharpening the difference not only between two kinds of knowledge but between two kinds of people.

Besides intensifying class differences, the stress discourse can increase the feelings of powerlessness that some analysts see as a major problem for workers. If indeed lack of control in demanding situations contributes to occupational disease etiology,[59] then having to depend on outside professionals to describe workplace conditions could itself conceivably increase the incidence of those diseases. Similarly, by offering technological interpretations of human experiences, stress research contributes in its own small way to the technocratic, high-speed, machine-paced society that may play a causal role in chronic illness.

The third argument against the stress discourse is that social problems at the workplace lend themselves poorly to scientific investigation. Clearly, as the public records of the PATCO strike show, science was not kind to the air traffic controllers. The studies introduced during the congressional hearings undermined to the point of collapse the controllers' contention that their jobs were intrinsically stressful. The scientific reports made job stress into a private, individual experience; seriously questioned a causal connection between air traffic control and either physical or emotional health; and suggested that, since its consequences are hard to demonstrate, the stress the controllers talked about may not even exist.

The controllers had little with which to counter these conclusions, not only because they lacked comparable resources to commission their own research, but because any other studies, were they to go beyond merely correlating disease and air traffic control, would resemble the Rose study.[60] Following behavioral science's canons, such studies would be forced to break down the job into empirical and quantifiable elements, and thus they too would likely conclude that the stress problem is essentially individual. Limited by the tools available to science, other studies would probably repeat the Rose study's inability to demonstrate a clear causal relation between the work of air traffic control and disease.

The Rose report itself provides the key to understanding this. In a remark quoted twice earlier in this chapter, its authors, ironically enough, call up the hermeneutic insistence that human affairs are only explicable in terms of meaning. "The stress level," they said, "is determined in part by the psychological and physiological 'interpreters' of the individual."[61] Other stress researchers have come to the same conclusion. As early as the 1950s Harold Wolff pointed out that stress is fundamentally subjective. It is, he said, "the meaning of the stimuli [that] makes them assume the nature of 'stress.'"[62]

Unfortunately, science cannot investigate meaning. It has no tools for interpreting social events. It can only measure objective phenomena. Based firmly on the assumption that an objective study of empirical reality is the only way to truth, science falls short as an instrument with which to study social events. To put it another way, the fact that it has a meaning is precisely what distinguishes a social event from a physical object, but meaning is by definition subjective and thus inaccessible to classical scientific methodology. Of course this calls into question all of social science; and indeed, social science today is in the throes of a quiet rebellion, the outcome of which is not yet known. Some social scientists see their discipline fundamentally challenged by the critique.[63] As the vigor of stress research demonstrates, however, powerful conservative forces still support the seductive belief that social science can eventually discover and effectively apply objective, rational, and precise knowledge to all social problems.

It is exactly this hope and this promise that attracted the air traffic controllers to the stress discourse; yet their faith was ill founded. The point here is not to impugn stress research as an embodiment of science because it poorly served the interests of controllers. If such research were able to describe jobs adequately, it would be valuable regardless of whether it led to pro-PATCO political decisions. The point is that science, because it disaggregates the job and leaves out meaning, necessarily fails to represent it completely.

The mistake the air traffic controllers made was to bring up the term *stress* in the first place. Given the way that the stress discourse can be employed to confuse the issue, to individualize job conditions, and to blame workers for their diseases and emotional discomforts, the controllers should have stuck to ordinary language. They should have argued only that their jobs are demanding, anxiety-producing, and tense. They should have insisted that in saying this they were merely describing their jobs as they knew them and that they were not making a case for anything about which science has any particular expertise. They should have contended that a decent respect for working people requires that such demanding, tense, and difficult jobs be rewarded better (or be made less trying). They should have avoided the temptation to enlarge upon the importance of these experiences by claiming that they also have negative physical, emotional, and social outcomes, for they should have reasoned that job-related pathologies would decrease along with reduced demand and tension. In short, the controllers should have made every effort to keep the discussion about job conditions on a nonscientific level. Once they let experts enter the discussion, their battle was lost.

CHAPTER 6

Vietnam Veterans and Agent Orange

It may not be surprising to find that when a social situation is blamed for disease, investigators have a hard time disentangling objective from subjective phenomena. Their politics easily get in the way of their science. But one might assume that when causality is ascribed to a chemical, science can clearly be distinguished from politics. This chapter examines that assumption, taking as a case in point the toxicity of dioxin.

During the Vietnam War, the United States military sprayed ten million gallons of an herbicide called Agent Orange over the Vietnamese countryside, exposing unknown numbers of American troops as well as Vietnamese soldiers and civilians to a substance that is extraordinarily toxic to animals. Now, many of these people have developed serious diseases including cancer and have produced children with divers birth defects. Believing that Agent Orange caused these illnesses and defects, a group of American veterans and their families sued the herbicide manufacturers in 1979. An out-of-court settlement in May 1984 awarded the veterans $180 million. The defendants, however, do not acknowledge culpability, and neither the reports of the suit nor the many pages of concurrent congressional testimony makes clear whether or not Agent Orange damages human health. The chemical companies, the Department of Defense, and the Veterans' Administration still maintain that Agent Orange is not particularly dangerous. Veterans' organizations, along with a variety of public interest groups, maintain that it is.

What are we to make of this controversy? Is one side lying? Is one side honestly misinformed? Are both sides jumping to conclusions from insufficient data? Can any kind of impartial policy ever be fashioned from this conflict? Let me begin to answer these questions by considering the usual way the U.S. media portray environmental and occupational health policy making. First, a problem is suspected: a new chemical, or a familiar one previously considered safe, is revealed (sometimes because of amateur sleuthing, usually because of preliminary professional studies) as a possible threat to health. Second, scientists, applying more rigorous methodology, search out the facts about the toxicity of the substance and determine what degree of risk it poses for the public. Third, policy makers enter the picture. They take these scientific facts, mix in some political reality based on their knowledge of interest groups, and propose a regulation. The proposal is tossed around in public hearings (which result in more modifications owing to the addition of a bit more political reality), and finally a new policy emerges.

That is not how it happens, though. In the first place, the problem is seldom exclusively the health effects of substances. In the second place, the facts are rarely clear. In the third place, there is no unambiguous distinction between scientists (neutral, objective) and policy makers (guided largely by political and economic considerations), nor between either of these and interest groups (influenced by ideology or self-gain). Instead, science, politics, and ideology interact with one another. This interaction, neither lamentable nor corrigible, is the cardinal fact about policy making. Understanding policy arguments requires a conception of this interaction.

FACTS AND MEANING

Agent Orange was the most heavily used of six herbicides sprayed by U.S. troops on Vietnam between 1962 and 1970. Named for the orange band marking the fifty-five-gallon drums in which it was stored, Agent Orange was composed of two principal chemicals: 2,4-D (dichlorophenoxyacetic acid) and 2,4,5-T (trichlorophenoxyacetic acid). It also contained a third chemical, 2,3,7,8-tetrachlorodibenzo-*p*-dioxin, or TCDD, usually referred to as dioxin, an unavoidable contaminant produced in the manufacture of 2,4,5-T. All three chemicals are toxic, but dioxin is extraordinarily so. Even in extremely minute doses, it has a pronounced effect on laboratory animals, damaging the liver, suppressing cell-mediated immunity, and causing birth defects and hepatic cancer.[1]

About 90 percent of the Agent Orange in Vietnam was used to defoliate trees and shrubs in order to deny the enemy ground cover. An additional 8 percent was used for crop destruction, and the remaining 2 percent killed weeds around base camps, cache sites, water ways, and communication lines. Most of the spraying was carried out by the air force in a program dubbed Operation Ranch Hand that employed fixed-wing aircraft. Smaller amounts were sprayed from helicopters, boats, trucks, and backpacks.[2]

By their own account, the U.S. military considered Agent Orange an insignificant health hazard. It issued no warnings, and evidently no personnel took safety precautions.[3] Indeed, according to reports from former GIs, air force herbicide handlers not uncommonly became drenched with the stuff, either from mishaps of one sort or another or from playful spray fights. In addition, ground troops sometimes entered newly sprayed areas, inevitably brushing up against foliage. They also drank water from streams and ponds after the sprayers had been through, ate food in the area, went swimming, and inhaled burning brush.[4] In the base camps, troops transformed empty Agent Orange drums into hibachis and latrines and incorporated them into bunkers, runways, and paths.[5]

No one seriously contradicts any of this. What the court case, the congressional hearings, and the scientific literature do question is whether, given this exposure, the former military men and women are now at risk for disease. Can the cancers, other chronic illnesses, and birth defects be attributed to Agent Orange? It seems a straightforward question, but when scientists reply, they give contradictory answers. Some agree with the Vietnam veterans' groups, saying that Agent Orange (or its contaminant, dioxin) is dangerous to humans. Some agree with the chemical companies, the Veterans' Administration, and the Department of Defense, saying it is not.

For example, a study by air force scientists on the Ranch Hand personnel concluded that current evidence is "insufficient to support a [causal] relationship between herbicide exposure and adverse health."[6] Scientists at the Centers for Disease Control (CDC) announced that their research on the children of Vietnam veterans showed "no support . . . for the proposition that Vietnam veterans (in general) have been at different risk than other men for fathering babies with the types of birth defects that we studied."[7] In addition, the American Medical Association says, "Thus far, long-term effects, except for persistent chloracne, have not been seen [in people exposed to dioxin]."[8] And Philip Abelson, former editor of *Science*, wrote that there is no "ironclad proof . . . for believing that TCDD is a dangerous carcinogen in humans. It is clear that, when administered orally, TCDD is highly toxic, but when bound to soil it does not pose much of a hazard."[9]

In contrast, an editorial in the *Journal of the American Medical Association* says that studies on workers exposed to dioxin reveal a higher than normal incidence of a rare cancer called soft-tissue sarcoma and of porphyria cutanea tarda, a liver condition. "Other reports have noted that workers fatigued easily and experienced weight loss, myalgias, insomnia, irritability, and decreased libido. The liver has been shown to become tender and enlarged and sensory changes, particularly in the lower extremities, have been reported."[10] Similarly, a study by the National Institute for Occupational Safety and Health "suggests . . . a range of toxic effects associated with TCDD exposure in man, especially heavily exposed workers. . . . Preliminary data collected by NIOSH suggest a possible association between occupational exposure to TCDD and an increased number of deaths from soft-tissue sarcoma."[11] Investigations in Sweden also "showed an increased risk for soft tissue sarcoma related to the use of phenoxyacetic acids or chlorophenols."[12] And other data indicate that women exposed to dioxin experience "a sharp increase in spontaneous abortions during the first trimester . . . and significant increases in risk of malformations."[13]

This clash of scientific studies puts Agent Orange in the same category as acid rain, radiation, formaldehyde, and ethylene dibromide (EDB). It calls up Love Canal, Three Mile Island, and Seveso. For all of these and other cases of suspect substances in the occupational and ambient environment, people presumably at risk are alternately reassured and alarmed by conflicting news stories of the danger. For all of these, too, the scientific literature displays a controversy among scientists about the degree to which the public's health is endangered. Not only do the people who stand to gain and lose personally take opposing sides on these issues, but their positions represent an underlying scientific debate.

Were we discussing conflicting positions held by lawyers or politicians, the clergy, teachers, or even physicians, the fact of their disagreement would be neither disturbing nor puzzling. We expect these other professionals to argue. They received different educations, have different abilities, and adhere to different principles. But we put scientists in another category. Laypeople and scientists alike think that science is qualitatively different from the law, medicine, religion, and education. Unlike the other disciplines science seems to be a source of fact. We distinguish it by definition from emotionalism and bias, and we look to it to provide us with accurate statements about the world. Most people would agree with Galileo that "the conclusions of natural science are true and necessary, and the judgement of man has nothing to do with them."[14] Science provides certainties. "The method of scientific investigation," says T. H. Huxley, "is simply the mode at which all phenomena are reasoned about, rendered precise and exact."[15] "Science," echoes Jacob Bronowski "made its way not secretly and not by authority but by sticking to the plain facts and only the facts—never mind who discovered them or who challenged them."[16] And James Bryant Conant affirms, "There is no question that one of the necessary conditions for science is an excellent and impartial analysis of the facts."[17]

An understanding that science will cut through controversy and provide fact undergirds congressional hearings convened over many topics. Congresspeople conventionally exhort one another to eschew emotion and regard scientific facts. The dioxin hearings were no exception. For example:

> *Rep. Satterfield:* There is no doubt that Agent Orange is an extremely disturbing issue. Emotionalism and controversy have surrounded the subject since it first surfaced. . . . Facts are needed in order to allay possible fears of Vietnam veterans and their families.[18]

> *Rep. Heckler:* Now we should not consider the question of Agent Orange or the problems of the Vietnam veteran in a vacuum . . . I think we need high scientific inquiry, solid evidence, medical data, and we need some kind of response to the veteran.[19]

> *Rep. McGrath:* We need some answers and we need them based on sound scientific investigations so that we can resolve this dioxin controversy once and for all.[20]

> *Rep. Schneider:* Too much of the debate over dioxin has been based upon theory and upon speculation and, quite frankly, too little upon fact and scientific evidence.[21]

Similar affirmations about the ability of science to settle debates occur hearing after hearing, despite the reality that the scientists called on to deliver the facts inevitably disagree with one another. This contradiction between the belief that facts come from science and the knowledge that scientists provide opposing facts raises a pressing question: why do scientists disagree?

My earlier paragraphs on Agent Orange give one clue. In describing the Agent Orange issue, I necessarily made political decisions about how to present it. The above account assumes that the story of Agent Orange begins with the spraying, that the question is whether dioxin makes people sick, that Agent Orange is a military issue, and that the main goal is compensation. But there are other ways to frame the subject. Environmentalists, for example, see the Agent Orange story as only one chapter in a larger tale about the irresponsible production, marketing, and disposal of many toxic substances by American and multinational corporations. They begin the story in the 1950s with the Dow Chemical Company's development of 2,4,5-T and include in it the increasing contamination of the environment and the workplace. The veterans, in contrast, set the beginning of the story at the beginning of the war. For most of them, Agent Orange has little to do with the environment, and it is not synonymous with dioxin. To them, Agent Orange is a metaphor. It includes dioxin poisoning, but it mainly stands for their experiences in Vietnam. Their principal goal is not compensation for having been exposed, nor is it the reduction of other environmental contaminants. Instead they want the American public to recognize the sacrifices they made during the war.

Let me elaborate. Most of the veterans active in the Agent Orange issue joined the military out of patriotism. As the chairman of the National Veterans Task Force said proudly, "They were ordered by the government to risk life and death in an ill-defined carnage, and whether it was agreeable or not, they went where they were told and did what they were ordered to do."[22] Unlike the draft resisters, they forthrightly followed the rules. But when they got to Vietnam, they encountered a war not only brutal and full of horrors, like all wars, but aimless and demoralizing. They quickly realized the inapplicability of their training and the uselessness of their seemingly superior technology. They also saw that battles and maneuvers brought them no closer to any clear goal. There was no point to the danger and the deaths. For many, it was the first time they doubted their government's wisdom. They felt exploited and betrayed. Moreover, when they finally came home, they met disrespect. Instead of being honored for what they had endured, like veterans before them, they were blamed for the military failure. So they hid their participation, sometimes even from the people they subsequently married, and tried to readjust to everyday life.[23]

In the late 1970s the veterans' situation began to change. By then news stories about environmental toxins were common, new research on dioxin had followed industrial accidents, and dioxin began to be called the most toxic substance known to humankind. At the same time, some veterans were becoming ill with chronic diseases and producing deformed children. Certainly it is part of their story, too, that in 1980 the Americans held hostage in Iran came home to ticker tape parades and national adulation. Before that, however, a benefits counselor at the Chicago Veterans' Administration hospital had begun contacting government offices to find out whether the defoliants used in Vietnam could have caused some of the illnesses and deaths she had been seeing among veterans.[24]

All of this led a handful of people to reevaluate the veterans' situation in a medical light. Agent Orange, it appeared, could explain the veterans' diseases and their children's birth defects. In addition, it offered the means for veterans to receive the recognition they had been denied. The films, pamphlets, public speeches, press releases, and books on Agent Orange produced by and for veterans describe the herbicide in metaphors that recall the war itself: Agent Orange is "disguised," "insidious," "perplexing." It lies in wait for them; it "lurks"; it "ensnares." "Stalked by an unseen enemy," veterans are helpless to protect themselves and their families.[25] Moreover, they describe the effects of Agent Orange as extraordinary, as ailments that defy common categories, that cannot be explained even by the best informed people. As one sympathizer puts it:

> [Veterans] uniformly report their physicians were puzzled by their complaints. Physicians would continuously diagnose their problems only to rule, on the basis of conventional medical testing, that the suspected [agent] was not the cause. They uniformly report being issued prescription after prescription, none of which proved effective with any consistency. . . . Their ailments were so frequently undefinable by repeated medical tests that their physicians often gave up searching for the answers.[26]

A veteran whose child was born with several birth defects says, "Nicholas had every imaginable deformity. . . . What a strange feeling to know that my son is also a victim of war. The doctors cannot explain why, they only say he is the worst case they have ever seen."[27] And the head of a veterans' organization says:

> These people have two, three, four children with birth defects. The children don't have just up-front birth defects either. They have mysterious illnesses. They have crib deaths. But when they go out and have another baby, it has two, three, four birth defects. And amniocentesis does not work for us.
>
> . . . With chloracne, the body breaks into horrible pustules for no discernible reason. It's untreatable. . . . We get calls from doctors who say, "I've had this vet and I've done everything I can for him and he just keeps getting sicker, just keeps going down. Do you know anything more I can do?"[28]

Through such descriptions veterans and their supporters call on the rest of the nation to agree that veterans deserve attention for what they went through in Vietnam and for its physical and emotional consequences. They want recognition. They want treatment. And they want revenge. At one of the hearings for the Agent Orange suit, the wife of one veteran stated, "We do not ask for money but for the truth, for someone to admit what has been done and to try to stop what shall prove to be the beginning of a nation of mutations." And then she socked it to them: "Our sons and daughters shall join their mutated and damaged chromosomes with those perfect and pretty little offspring of you who went to law school and into corporate employ instead of to Da Nang, An Khe, and Quang Tri. We shall then be vindicated when our daily existence becomes your greatest nightmare."[29]

In addition to all of this, the veterans want meaning. Putting aside questions of the significance of the war itself, they want their actions there and the aftermath of those actions—the alienation and the pain—to have import. They want some measure of the honor bestowed upon previous generations of soldiers. In addition, they want an explanation for medical misfortunes, or rather, they want to understand cancer and birth defects and miscarriages and intractable illnesses not as personal misfortunes but as explicable events connected to something.[30]

By moving these events from the personal to the political realm, they hope to affirm that the world is orderly and that their lives make sense.

This is a way to understand the veterans' response to Agent Orange studies. The authors of the air force's Ranch Hand study and of CDC's birth defects study naively announced that veterans would be reassured to know that Agent Orange is safe. But the veterans were not. They rejected the studies' conclusions because the threat they posed to the larger issue canceled out the reassurance they were supposed to bring. Research showing that exposure to Agent Orange has no health effects deprives veterans of the recognition they seek and the meaning they desire. Having loaded both those weighty goals into the cart of science, veterans are in the peculiar position of hoping to learn that they —at least as a group—are at high risk for disease; for by establishing the risk, veterans also establish their right to be honored for what happened to them in Vietnam. In addition they get something few people can hope for: when they are sick, they have an answer to the question, Why me? Being sick equals being exploited and betrayed in Vietnam and therefore deserving special attention.

Such conflation of meanings occurs in other cases too. After the 1976 explosion of a chemical plant in Seveso, Italy, many residents refused to act as though dioxin were dangerous. They disobeyed orders and kept returning to the evacuated areas at night, repeatedly tearing down fences and mocking the moon-suited decontamination workers. Frustrated authorities attributed this behavior to stupidity. But, according to one writer, for the residents, obeying the rules had a political meaning: "Cleaning up, sweeping away dioxin, meant sweeping away many other things: the corruption, inefficiency and the inadequacy of the Christian Democratic regime."[31] The same can be said about Love Canal. To cap the canal has, for some, come to mean disposing of the problem. It is not merely an ineffective way to contain waste. It also seems to relieve the dumpers and the health authorities of responsibility for the contamination in the first place.[32] In cases like these, however much people may want their own lives to be healthy, they also want disease, because it exhibits injustice.

SCIENTIFIC DISAGREEMENT

All this may explain why veterans disagree with negative studies on Agent Orange, but it does not at first appear to explain why scientists disagree with one another. Why do scientists disagree? Inevitably, a body of literature exists to answer the question. The answers fall into four categories. Some are ad hominem, dwelling on the characteristics of the opposing scientists. Some are dualistic, pointing out a confusion between science and politics. Some are procedural, concentrating on a lack of consensus about rules of evidence. Some are epistemological, analyzing the social context of scientific knowledge. I now briefly discuss each of these in turn.

The ad hominem explanation actually seldom appears in a formal analysis of scientific disagreement. Instead it is implicit in the predominant understanding that science is neutral. If science is a method for uncovering facts, the scientist is only a vehicle for their discovery. Thus if one scientist's facts seem to disagree with another's, something must be wrong with one of the scientists. Or something may be wrong with a whole group of scientists—all industry scientists, for example, or scientists in a certain university laboratory, or in one particular government agency. Those people, this tacit reasoning goes, suffer from one or more of three faults: (1) They are liars. They do fraudulent work, are deliberately dishonest, either covering up inconvenient data or inventing information. (2) They are incompetent. They do shoddy work, are careless. They contaminate cultures, forget to feed their rats, lose their notes, design dumb questionnaires, or make erroneous calculations. (3) They are politically biased. They consciously and unfairly produce work to support the interests of one party or the other.

Such accusations may on occasion be valid. Incompetent and dishonest scientists do exist. They even work in very prestigious institutions.[33] But given that in any scientific debate both sides are likely to charge their opponents with these faults, the ad hominem explanation is not convincing. At least it does not explain enough. In any hotly debated issue, each side can also produce good studies by respected scientists. So the (inevitable) presence of a few disreputable researchers cannot account for scientific disagreement. In fact, most analysts of scientific disagreement recognize this, whether or not the average scientist does. It is because they discard the ad hominem argument that they look for other explanations.

The second, the dualistic, explanation sees disagreements among researchers as misunderstandings about the boundaries of science. Some scientists, the reasoning goes, confuse science and policy making. According to this view, disagreements among scientists would diminish if scientists confined their attention to science and handed over to policy makers the question of what the science means. Ian Clark, in an analysis of the controversy about supersonic transport, articulates the position: "It is possible to distinguish purely "technical questions" from the "questions of policy" in any issue. . . . Experts should make this distinction explicit and should have no greater voice in the resolution of policy than the ordinary citizen or layman."[34]

In a somewhat different formulation of this viewpoint, Alvin Weinberg proposes a category he calls "trans-scientific." Rejecting the notion of a clear line between science and politics, he offers in its stead a clear line between science and trans-science. The former deals with questions of "truth," "unambiguously answerable" by "strict scientific canons." The latter deals with three other sorts of questions: those that "would be impractically expensive" to answer with the scientific method (because they require, say, a billion rats or a hundred years); those for which "the subject matter is too variable" (the prediction of individual human behavior as opposed to group or average behavior); and those which "themselves involve moral and aesthetic judgements."[35]

Anyone who attends congressional hearings or who reads

their records knows that scientists do indeed offer opinions about policy. That much is clear. But it is not at all obvious that the spheres of science and policy, or science and "trans-science," are separable. Like the ad hominem explanation for scientific disagreement, the dualistic explanation rests on a belief that an external world of objective events is empirically distinguishable from the internal subjectivity of the person apprehending it. But even the proponents of this sort of dualism recognize weaknesses in the underlying assumption. Implicitly admitting that the distinction is hard to maintain, Clark says that opposing forces in the SST debate rarely divorced science from policy. And Weinberg notes that "often the line between science and trans-science is blurred: in fact, the essence of the matter is often to define just where the line between the two lies."[36] Here he undermines his whole case, at least if his goal is conflict reduction. Arguments among scientists cannot be reduced by adhering to a distinction between science and something that is not science unless the distinction can be made.

The third and fourth explanations for scientific disagreements differ from the first two. They look not at the scientist but at science. In varying degrees they suggest that we find scientific disagreement problematic because we have an incorrect idea of what science is. Scientists disagree because science, instead of being neutral, yields a variety of legitimate answers, depending on how scientists use it. Analysts who put forward what I am calling the procedural explanation for disagreement show that while science includes many precisely defined methodologies with explicit rules for their utilization, no metarules tell scientists which methodology or which rule to apply to a given problem. Thus according to this explanation, debates among scientists derive from differences about which methods or rules are appropriate for answering the question at hand.

For example, Evans's paper on the many modifications of the classic Henle-Koch postulates shows that some controversies can be attributed to conflicting ideas about the rules of causality. Even though Koch himself never regarded his postulates as rigid criteria, some scientists do. They can argue endlessly about the evidence necessary to determine that a substance is the cause of a disease.[37]

In an article explaining why the United States and Great Britain take opposing positions about the carcinogenicity of aldrin and dieldrin, Gillespie et al. show that each government simply accepted different rules of evidence. The United States calls these pesticides carcinogenic because it held to the rule that any substance carcinogenic to a single animal species will also be considered carcinogenic to humans. Great Britain, in contrast, says these are not carcinogenic, a determination based on its rule that a substance will be considered carcinogenic to humans only if there is evidence of tumor formation from more than one species plus a "reliable" demonstration that the animals' response is analogous to the human response.[38] And Reisor points out that the early controversies over the connection between cigarette smoking and disease were basically debates about whether direct laboratory testing is necessary to demonstrate causality or whether statistical data alone are adequate.[39]

The Agent Orange debate easily illustrates the procedural explanation for disagreement. The congressional hearings contain page after page of arguments by scientists about the rules of evidence. They show that, to agree on whether or not Vietnam veterans are at special risk for disease, scientists first have to agree on what kind of information demonstrates a health hazard. Consider just the question of whether or not Agent Orange causes cancer. How do we know if a substance is carcinogenic? There are three sources of information: experiments on laboratory animals, surveys of people presumably exposed, and in vitro tests with bacteria. None gives unequivocal answers. In the case of studies on laboratory animals, scientists do not simply expose rats to a suspected substance and then label it carcinogenic if the rats get cancer. Some substances cause tumors in mice but not in rats, or in mice and rats but not rabbits, or in none of these but in frogs. Some substances cause tumors in males but not in females, or vice versa. Some substances cause tumors in extremely minute doses in one species but only in much higher doses in another species. Some substances cause tumors when administered to the lungs but not when administered to the blood. In addition, a substance can cause tumors of the colon, say, in one species but only tumors of the stomach in another. To complicate the issue further, some substances cause benign tumors, whereas others cause malignant tumors; and some substances evidently cause tumors all by themselves, whereas others seem to require that something else happen first. With all this variation, the only legitimate answer to the question whether a substance causes cancer is, "It depends on the rules of evidence."

The acceptability of in vitro tests and human population studies similarly requires rules. In vitro tests are a particularly good example because they do not, in fact, even directly test for cancer. They are mutagen tests, acceptable in the first place only to scientists who agree with the rule that if a substance causes changes in the DNA, it will also be assumed to cause cancer. Similarly, to accept the result of epidemiological studies on human populations, scientists have to agree on previous questions. For example, can information about one group of people be applied to a second group who have different characteristics and different kinds of exposures? How can we say that a particular substance causes cancer when there is a lag time of up to forty years between the time of exposure and formation of tumors, when the substance leaves no recoverable traces in the body, and when nothing about a case of chemically induced cancer distinguishes it from a case of nonchemically induced cancer? By what rules can we show that a substance causes a particular kind of cancer when very few people get cancer from exposure to any of the known carcinogens and when there is a large "natural" or "background" number of identical cancers not traceable to any exposure? These questions all get answered. Scientific convention addresses some of them, and government regulatory agencies determine their rules of evidence for the rest.[40] But these are only customs; nothing inherent in the rules compels their adoption. Dissident scientists can always disagree.

Described this way, the debates about Agent Orange seem to uphold the proceduralists' explanation for scientific disagreement: that we can best understand such conflicts as debates over rules. But all I have really done here is describe the substance of scientific dispute. It is true that in the Agent Orange debates some scientists held that positive animal data, even in one species, were presumptive of human carcinogenicity and others held that they were not. Likewise, some scientists insisted that data on workers were applicable to Vietnam veterans while others insisted they were not; and some scientists claimed that data on air force personnel were applicable to ground troops, while others claimed they were not. But none of this tells us why scientists disagree over what facts are relevant and what rules should be followed. It does, though, approach an explanation that can tell us.

I call it the epistemological explanation because it rests on arguments by philosophers of science that science is not a special form of knowledge. Like other fields, science is a product of society, and scientists do not pursue a category of inquiry radically different from the humanities. This explanation for scientific disagreement builds on the proposition that positivism, the basis of science, is an ideology. It impugns the dominant Western belief that fact and value, objective and subjective, mind and body are separate spheres, maintaining instead that we cannot separate our selves from what we know. There is, these philosophers argue, no presuppositionless knowledge of the world; we perceive it through our culture. The best known among them, Thomas Kuhn, shows that what scientists take to be normal science—the paradigm that underlies their work—changes over time. And when paradigms change, so do facts. It is not precisely true, he says, that the world is fixed and only our interpretation of it changes. Instead in a complex sense we change the world when we look at it in a new way. The concept is counterintuitive, at least among Western people, and Kuhn tries to elucidate it:

> The world that the student . . . enters . . . is determined jointly by the environment and the particular normal-science tradition that the student has been trained to pursue. Therefore, at times of

revolution, when the normal-scientific tradition changes, the scientist's perception of his environment must be re-evaluated—in some familiar situations he must learn to see a new gestalt. After he has done so the world of his research will seem, here and there, incommensurable with the one he had inhabited before.[41]

He goes on to affirm that although "the world does not change with a change of paradigm, the scientist afterward works in a different world . . . I am convinced that we must learn to make sense of statements that at least resemble these."[42]

Another philosopher of science, Stephen Toulmin, even more strongly makes the case that science is an interaction between the scientist and the things he or she looks at. It became clear in the early twentieth century, he asserts, that "the standpoint of the detached onlooker, from which—in theory at least—classical scientists had observed and speculated about the world, was no more than an abstraction."[43] He argues that while the sciences and the humanities were once held to be incommensurable, "in recent decades, the whole basis for this contrast has been largely eroded. With the recognition that all scientific observation involves two-way interaction between the observer and the system being observed, we are no longer entitled even to treat material objects in a purely objectified manner."[44]

Feminists present some of the more provocative analyses of the interaction between scientists and the world they perceive. Arguing that scientists make observations in light of unconscious cultural assumptions, they claim that a masculine view of society pervades science. For example, Evelyn Fox Keller says that scientists usually describe what they observe—whether cells or groups of animals—in terms of domination or subordination. Women, she observes, whether scientists or not, tend to think in terms of horizontal relations and of dialectical processes. She shows that, until Barbara McClintock's work on DNA was taken seriously, scientists thought the DNA function was to encode and transmit the instructions for cell growth. McClintock's research challenged that hierarchical idea, producing instead " a view of DNA in delicate interaction with the cellular environment—an organismic view. . . . No longer is a master control to be found in a single component of the cells; rather control resides in the complex interaction of the entire system."[45] Michael Mulkay also argues that scientists inevitably draw on nonscientific assumptions to give order to what they observe. The work of a number of writers, he says, shows "that the formulation of scientific facts depends on prior commitments of various kinds, that these commitments are often made in accordance with participants' position in a specific social setting, and that they influence the informal acts of interpretation which are essential to give meaning to observations."[46] He points out that scientists need some previous assumptions to know how to recognize a pertinent fact and how to decide on the rules of evidence. They even need previous understandings to name something as a problem in the first place: "Scientists' choice of a particular definition of a technical problem cannot itself be decided by observation and systematic inference alone. Rather, it *precedes and is presupposed* in observation and analysis."[47]

The proposition that we cannot know reality objectively does not mean that we only know it subjectively—that anything goes, for everything is relative. Instead the point is that the actual world around us (which exists regardless of our inability to know it objectively) is not static and fixed. It is not something "discoverable," immaculate and separable from its discoverers. The world influences the way we see it, and the way we see it, in turn, influences the world. In other words, proponents of this school argue, we must develop a dialectical view of reality. Since reality is in essence an interrelationship between subjective and objective phenomena, then no purely nonhuman perspective is ever possible. We can only approximate an ever-changing truth.

If these philosophers are right, there is no neutral, strictly "scientific" answer to the question of whether Agent Orange causes disease and birth defects. Or, more precisely, scientists can never discover a neutral answer. All answers will be partly subjective. They will include values. Thus, if scientists eventually agree, it will not be because they will have found the unequivocal truth. Neither will it be because they have rid their ranks of dishonest researchers, learned to separate science from policy, or adopted the same rules. Instead it will be because they have agreed to apply similar values to the issue. Then some ways of defining it will become illegitimate and others will become appropriate: some rules of evidence will be admitted and others barred. This subtle and intricate change will occur, if it does, because both new research and a new political climate will emerge. And each of these will affect the other.

VALUES IN SCIENCE

Consider the effect of values on three aspects of Agent Orange research: how scientists determine what facts are pertinent, how they design their studies, and how they interpret them when they are finished. First, as far as the facts are concerned, scientists have many choices. They have the option to restrict the pertinent data to the effect of dioxin on the physical health of veterans, to include in the pertinent data the effect of dioxin on the physical health of workers and other civilians, to widen the definition of pertinent data even more and count the effect of dioxin on the health of laboratory animals, or to extend the definition to incorporate the emotional consequences of serving in Vietnam. Each of these options produces a different definition of the issue, and all the possible definitions are perfectly legitimate. But the first option is likely to show that dioxin is not particularly dangerous because veterans were initially inducted into the service partly on the basis of their presumed resistance to disease and because they were still young. The second option is somewhat more likely to show that dioxin is dangerous because workers might have received larger doses than the average veteran. The third option will definitely show dioxin to be toxic, but the degree of toxicity will depend on the animal species. And the last option, because "emotional consequences" can mean almost anything, can be used for any purposes. How do scientists decide which option to pursue? There is no purely objective choice. Scientists have to mix objective and subjective knowledge. Despite a desire to keep science separate from politics, scientists must turn to their values to help them define the pertinent facts. They have to decide whether they hope to prove dioxin safe or hazardous.

Scientists' values also influence their choice of methodology. For example, at a 1986 professional meeting, a scientist from the State University of New York at Binghamton suggested that no adequate control group for Agent Orange studies exists in the United States or Europe because dioxin is ubiquitous in industrial societies. He announced preliminary plans for a study on the health of southern Vietnamese (who, apparently as a result of the war, have average levels of dioxin in their fatty tissue three times that of Americans), using northern Vietnamese as a control group.[48] The study may or may not show that dioxin is a health hazard, but it is the kind of extensive inquiry a scientist designs who is dissatisfied with the conclusion that dioxin is safe. The comparatively simpler epidemiological studies usually done on populations in the United States inevitably show, this scientist believes, that moderate exposure to dioxin is safe simply because everybody here is already exposed. Displaying a similar intent to protect people from dioxin, two scientists at the National Institute of Occupational Safety and Health doggedly combined the results of several studies on workers which, taken individually, had shown dioxin to be safe. The aggregation of studies indicated the opposite.[49]

Values also influence the way scientists interpret their research. In explaining the meaning of their results, reputable scientists always practice caution because they never have quite enough data and because their research is never perfectly designed. But caution itself is not neutral. If an (inevitably) flawed study shows a substance to be toxic, it is cautious on behalf of the substance to reject the study but cautious on behalf of potentially exposed people to accept it. In contrast, if another (inevitably) imperfect study shows the substance to be benign, it is cautious on behalf of potentially exposed people to reject it but cautious on behalf of the substance to accept it. Many scientists hope to escape this dilemma by neither accepting nor rejecting studies. Instead they call for more. Because most research examines suspected hazards already in the environment, however, there is nothing neutral about suggesting they stay there until more data are collected. So every interpretation scientists make about these results reflects their values. Each indicates a commitment either to people or to substances.

To recapitulate, since there is a variety of legitimate facts, methods, and interpretations, scientists have to choose among them according to their assumptions, however unconscious, about what is valuable and about the political and social implications of their research. "All areas of scientific research," Mulkay reminds us,

> are characterized by situations in which the established technical cultures permit the formulation of several reasonable alternatives, none of which can be shown conclusively to be more correct than another. It is in making choices between such alternatives, whether at the level of broad definition of the problem or at the level of detailed analysis, that scientists' political commitments and the pressures of the political context come into play most clearly.[30]

Let us look more closely at the political context of the Agent Orange debate. The above observations suggest that scientists may be as influenced by politics as are veterans. Agent Orange, after all, is not an isolated issue. It willy-nilly represents two larger questions: do Vietnam veterans have a special claim on our attention, and does the physical environment pose a threat to health? On the one hand, a scientific agreement that Agent Orange is not toxic to humans would mean refusing Vietnam veterans extra treatment at the Veterans' Administration, denying them compensation from chemical companies, and negating their insight into the reasons for diseases and birth defects. It would also raise hopes that other suspect substances may also be safe. It would signify confidence in the U.S. military, in chemical companies, and in government regulatory agencies. It would support the presumption that we wage war sensibly and that we design industrial plants, dispose of chemicals, and run regulatory agencies in ways that protect health. The agreement would strengthen the impression that people who worry about chemicals are usually misinformed. It would support the idea that fear is the problem, not chemicals, and that the real issue is how to manage people, not how to manage technology.

On the other hand, if scientists were to agree that Agent Orange is a health hazard, then Vietnam veterans would receive different treatment from the Veterans' Administration and be entitled to more respect from the rest of us. In addition the claim that the environment is a significant source of disease would be strengthened. From this would follow, at the very least, suspicion of the Department of Defense, pressure on industry to change production materials and methods, and pressure on government to pass and enforce stronger regulations. It could do more. It could force a reappraisal of the benefits of advanced technology and legitimize calls for more citizen participation in decision making.

Certainly, good scientists try to bracket off their social knowledge about these possible consequences. And they should. But their social knowledge informs their values. The commitments they must call on to help define the issue, choose a methodology, and interpret the results spring from the political context in which they live and work. As long as scientists divide over the preferred social outcome of their work, they will disagree over what values are appropriate to employ in making these seemingly scientific decisions and therefore disagree about the toxicity of chemicals. But the disagreement is even more complicated than that. The toxicity of chemicals affects values, too. In a dialectical process—one not possible to capture precisely because it is never static—if studies accumulate showing that dioxin and other chemicals endanger human health, so too will a distrust of chemical companies' and government's claim to protect health. The shift in opinion, affecting scientists as well as the public, will influence the presuppositions scientists hold. Conversely, an accumulation of studies showing that dioxin and other chemicals are safe will contribute to an equally intricate dialectical process in which most people, including scientists, have confidence in industry and in government.

Which of these scenarios is more likely is the topic of the next chapter. It discusses the source of the unexamined ideas mixed into science; for while values influence science, scientists do not choose the values they bring to their work as freely as they decide among ice cream cone flavors. Usually, the extrascientific judgments that help them select the pertinent facts, the appropriate methodology, and the most reasonable interpretation match their society's predominant values. It is precisely because these values are so uncritically accepted that they appear to be objective facts.

CHAPTER 7

Individualism and Science

How will we finally come to think about the environment? The question takes us back to the opening chapters of this book. The politics of prevention is the struggle over the assignment of meaning to suspected causes of disease, for the political meaning that a causal statement acquires largely determines what kinds of prevention policies a society develops. Will "environmental hazards" bring to mind microparticles much like viruses and bacteria, or uncontrollable industrial production? Will "occupational stress" come to mean terrible job conditions or tense workers? Will the debate about smoking concern individual choice to enjoy a cigarette or forced exposure to toxic substances? Will the popular literature about unhealthy diets mainly discuss unscrupulous advertisers, or will it concentrate on inadequate health education? In short, will disease prevention policies place responsibility on individuals or on institutions and structures in the wider society?

Vested interests have power to influence answers to some of these questions. So, of course, does scientific research. Indeed the belief that we can rely on science to tell us how to think about disease causality allays the public's worry about the vested interests. The editor of *Science* promotes just that attitude in a 1986 editorial about the environment: "Environmentalists argue that we are doing too little to protect our resources; industry argues that excessive regulation stifles progress. The reality is that [the problems] cannot be solved by headlines, law cases, or political posturing." He goes on to advocate more basic research and a tripling of the EPA budget. "I would like to believe," he concludes, that "reason and data can be used to make decisions."[1] But as we have seen, there is no easy distinction between scientists on the one hand, employing reason and data, and environmentalists and industry on the other hand, arguing, creating headlines, going to court, and "posturing." The editor of *Science* himself is posturing here. But more interesting, his essay illustrates a widespread presumption about what science is, a presumption with its roots in political ideology. This final chapter is about that ideology. More powerful than vested interests, more subtle than science, political ideology has, in the end, the greatest influence on disease prevention policy.

Political ideology can mean several things. For many people an ideology is a set of beliefs that obscure or distort the truth. In popular parlance the term usually refers to a strong belief system that prevents people from looking dispassionately at new or different ideas. Thus Communists are accused of holding ideologies. So are members of certain religious groups. In academic usage, the term, construed negatively like this, means a collection of imposed and mistaken beliefs that create a false consciousness. Unexamined and taken for granted, these beliefs impel people to accept uncritically current political and economic arrangements even though those arrangements may not be in their interest. The concept is usually traced to Marx and Engels: "The ideas of the ruling classes are, in every epoch, the ruling ideas."[2]

A second meaning for ideology, one less concerned about deviations from the truth, defines it as a world view or a frame of reference. All people have relatively unconscious "beliefs about the present nature of the world and . . . hopes . . . for it," say Kenneth and Patricia Dolbeare. "Such beliefs and hopes, when integrated into a more or less coherent picture of (1) how the present social, economic, and political order operates, and (2) why this is so, and whether it is good or bad, and (3) what should be done about it, if anything, may be termed an 'ideology.'"[3]

This definition goes back to Karl Mannheim, who argued that ideology is a neutral concept: "The thought of all parties in all epochs is of an ideological character." Social scientists should not look for false ways of thought but should try to understand a social group's "structure of consciousness." Instead of judging a people's beliefs as right or wrong, one should "analyze . . . all the factors in the . . . social situation which may influence thought."[4] Georg Lukács elaborates on Mannheim's concept. The consciousness of any social group is a product of its history and experiences, he argues. This understanding "does not permit us to simply persist in an unflexible confrontation of true and false. On the contrary, it requires us to investigate this 'false consciousness' concretely as an aspect of the historical totality and as a stage in the historical process."[5]

Much of this book has been influenced by this second view of ideology. Indeed in what follows I discuss more forthrightly than I have up to this point the ways that two beliefs, individualism and reductionism, affect disease prevention policies. I make the case that the dominant modes of thought in the United States lead most Americans to conceive of disease causality in ways that steer prevention policies away from the most effective actions. But I then ask whether a study of ideology gets us to the most important issues about disease causality.

INDIVIDUALISM

While in any society people hold a variety of ideologies, one belief system tends to predominate, except during times of radical internal clashes. In the United States, the principle ideology usually goes under the rubric of individualism. Originally a collection of political theories carefully delineated by philosophers as explanations for the world they experienced, these propositions have in the fullness of time tended to lose their theoretical nature and become for many people simple facts.

Unlike the philosophies it derives from, individualism, in concert with all political ideologies, has no obvious texts. To study the *philosophy* of David Hume, or John Locke, or Thomas

Hobbes, one goes back to their writings. To study the *ideology* that these philosophers' ideas have popularly been reduced to, one can look for its cultural expressions, for culture both reflects and perpetuates political ideology. Ideology is displayed in popular culture—in films, the media, stories, advertisements, children's games, and so on. It is evident in distinctions between the sorts of acts that require explanation and the sorts that are treated as unproblematic. It shows up in the kinds of explanations problematic actions receive. It can be found by considering the organization of the dominant institutions, the structure of the law, or the assignment of responsibility. In short, all analyses of societies can discover unconscious assumptions.[6]

The classic description of the dominant American ideology, however, uses none of these methods. Steven Lukes's *Individualism* does not try to prove the existence of individualism by discovering it in society; he merely describes, simply and clearly, what most Americans believe about the nature of human beings and the ideal structure of society.[7] He roots these beliefs firmly in philosophy and does not discuss the subtle ways that culture, politics, economics, or law prompt and maintain them. In fact, he calls these beliefs "doctrines," not ideologies. But doctrines differ little from ideologies, for both are theories that people erroneously treat as facts. So Lukes provides a useful description of what most Americans believe about the legitimate source of knowledge, the nature of human beings, and the structure of the ideal society. This section owes much to his book, especially his distinction between the confining doctrines of individualism and its emancipatory goals.

Modern societies like ours, with their emphasis on social change and on individual liberty, contrast sharply with feudal societies, which, for all their vaunted harmony and tradition, stressed (and do stress) stasis, hierarchy, and authoritarian control. Modern societies glorify personal autonomy and self-realization. Their politically liberal as well as their conservative citizens celebrate the possibilities of personal change and growth, the idea of equality among people and the desirability of individual expression. Today the normative goal, however distant, in both capitalist and socialist countries is to create and maintain such an environment that every citizen can develop to his or her highest potential. All members of the United Nations subscribe to the belief that each person is individually worthy and thus that all should be treated equally.[8] The elevating (if sexist) phrase "the dignity of man" captures these individualistic values and provides a central conviction to guide the development of a just social order. More, it is the ideals of individualism that have motivated and justified the nineteenth and twentieth centuries' worldwide resistance to imperialism, racism, and sexism.

Unfortunately, individualism is more than a great liberator. It fosters narcissistic permutations (e.g., the "human potential movement" of the 1970s); it produces some miserable consequences (e.g., autonomy can also mean loneliness and isolation); and it contains intrinsic contradictions (e.g., it frees people to exploit one another). Besides these corollaries to its ideals, individualism drags along, at least in the United States, a second and less felicitous group of conceptions. These, also known collectively as individualism, limit rather than expand human potential. In addition they constitute a set of ideas that hobble the development and implementation of effective disease prevention policies.

The elements of ideological individualism all stem from a prefatory assumption that there is such a thing as a human nature. It takes for granted that all individuals have set wants, needs, interests, and purposes. "The crucial point about this conception," says Lukes, "is that the relevant features of individuals . . . are assumed as given, independent of a social context."[9] Moreover, those relevant features are believed to be selfishness and competitiveness. Individualistic ideology assumes each person is essentially self-interested and motivated solely by a desire to gain pleasure and avoid pain. This idea stands in contrast to the view that people have no particular intrinsic nature but become humans, as distinguished from animals, through the process of living in society.

A number of other assumptions pertinent to the disease causality issue are linked to the core belief that human beings have an identifiable, selfish, and competitive nature. One is the assumption that individuals are the best judges of their own interests and that therefore governments should be confined to protecting individuals' rights and guarding their freedom to pursue their interests. Lukes contrasts this with the idea that government "might legitimately influence or alter [citizens'] wants, interpret their interests for them or invade or abrogate their rights."[10] The concept is similar to the idea that people are spiritually on their own and neither have nor need intermediaries between them and God. Indeed, Lukes suggests that the philosophy (not the ideology) of individualism was basically religious.[11]

Another important aspect of individualistic ideology is the belief that the individual is the supreme arbiter of morality. This means that, as Lukes puts it, "one should seek to secure one's own good, not that of society as a whole or of other individuals."[12] Lukes points out that this assumption leads logically to the idea that facts and values are distinct, for it makes values entirely personal, independent of any objective criterion which could make one value superior to any other. It thus relates to the idea that individual experience is the source of all knowledge. He argues that the doctrine is the foundation of empiricism, the belief at the heart of modern science. It takes for granted that sensory data are, or at least can be, received unmediated by social phenomena such as custom, prejudice, or language.

Finally, individualistic ideology assumes that the proper study of society concentrates on individuals. This view does not deny that "society" exists (we all recognize such wholes as armies, for example, that are irreducible to statements about soldiers), but it makes the individual its basic unit. It stands in opposition to holism and to either holistic or dialectical explanations for behavior. Individualism thus makes it reasonable to explain human activity with as little reference as possible to the abstract, the nonconcrete. Within this ideology, hard-to-measure phenomena like social class, intentions, and shared meaning become not quite "real."

Lukes's point in distinguishing the doctrines of individualism from the ideals of individualism is to show the contradiction between them. He argues, far more eloquently than I can indicate here, that we have to abandon most of the former if we hope to attain the latter. A commitment to liberty and equality, he says, requires us to think of individuals, not as embodiments of abstract characteristics and fillers of certain roles, but as concrete *persons* with multiple capacities. Similarly, a goal of egalitarian social change commits us to social analyses richer than the reductionist methodology consistent with individualism. That methodology, he says, "simply precludes one from examining the deeper structural and institutional forces which constitute the central obstacles to [egalitarian] change. [It] must clearly be rejected as not merely theoretically narrow, but as socially and politically regressive."[13]

This distinction between individualism as an ideal and individualism as a doctrine readily lends itself to an analysis of disease prevention policies. The *ideals* of individualism provide the ethical foundation for the kind of structurally based disease prevention policies discussed in chapter three because, were they well implemented, they would protect everyone's health. Thus they affirm the democratic and egalitarian goals central to philosophical individualism. But the *doctrines* of individualism—that is, individualism as an ideology—constitute a barrier to the attainment of the goals. Taking the doctrines for granted—considering them facts rather than theories—most people bring to the consideration of social problems unconscious presuppositions that bias them in favor of individualistic solutions. This means that most of the politics of policy making have already taken place by the time proposals reach the public agenda. It is already assumed that parts are distinct from wholes and that the parts are more important.

INDIVIDUALISM AND DISEASE PREVENTION POLICY

First, and most obvious, economic individualism and political individualism make government regulations perverse. In individualistic ideology, it is regulations that have to be justified, not the absence of regulations. Hiding behind the opposition to occupational and environmental health regulations is an argument that such regulations go against human nature. It is not just that they cost industries money and give government a measure of control over businesses. Rules seeking to safeguard health from harmful products and production processes seem to violate the natural order. Cherishing the conviction that men and women are the best judges of their own interests and that governments have no legitimate role in interpreting their interests for them, many people have what they view as an inborn opposition to health and safety regulations. So behind protests against laws that would force automobile manufacturers to make cars more crash worthy, require motorcyclists to wear helmets, ban the private possession of handguns, or prohibit soft drink companies from using saccharin, lie more than simple opposition to government regulation. The protests rest on the belief that regulations shackle the expression of human nature.

It is partly due to the strength of individualistic ideology that so few Americans realize that in all modern capitalist countries, governments promulgated regulations to protect public health as early as the beginning of the Industrial Revolution.[14] Surely even fewer know that the classical political economists, including Adam Smith and Nassau Senior, argued that the state must interfere when the market fails.[15] But given the power of the ideology, a better knowledge of history would make little difference. Government regulation of business would continue to seem, at best, just what those economists thought it was: a necessary evil.

Individualistic ideology supports a second position. It makes the individual the basic unit of social analysis. It supports a politically conservative predisposition to bracket off questions about the structure of society—about the distribution of wealth and power, for example—and to concentrate instead on questions about the behavior of individuals within that (apparently fixed) structure. One consequence is the assumption that health education is the best way to prevent disease. Unhealthy behavior results from individual choice, the ideology implies, so the way to change such behavior is to show people the error of their ways and urge them to act differently. Hidden behind statements that people themselves should be able to choose freely what to eat, whether to smoke, and how sedentary to be lies the ideological assumption that people are the best judges of their own interests. It begs the question of whether people actually are. Similarly, the opinion that it is all right for television stations to advertise junk food to children and cigarettes to adults is not just a defense of the First Amendment. It also reflects individualism's assumption that the individual is the final moral authority.

William Ryan criticizes individualistic thinking in his 1972 book *Blaming the Victim*.[16] He describes a health education poster about lead paint poisoning, a serious problem in slum housing when children commonly ingest bits of paint chips from poorly repainted walls and furniture. The poster explains that if children eat lead paint, they can suffer brain damage, become seriously ill, and even die. "Now, no one would argue against the idea," says Ryan, "that it is important to spread knowledge about the danger of eating paint in order that parents might act to forestall their children from doing so. But," he goes on,

> to campaign against lead paint *only* in these terms is destructive and misleading. . . . The cause of the poisoning is the lead in the paint on the walls of the apartment in which the children live. The presence of the lead is illegal. To use lead paint in a residence is illegal; to permit lead paint to be exposed in a residence is illegal. . . . To ignore these continued and repeated law violations, to ignore the fact that the supposed law enforcer actually cooperates in lawbreaking, and then to load a burden of guilt on the mother of a dead or dangerously ill child is an egregious distortion of reality.[17]

Of course one reason for assigning responsibility to individuals instead of to law enforcement agencies or landlords is that individual responsibility seems politically neutral. This is so because individualistic ideology politicizes categories beyond the individual level. "Will I get sick if this stuff is in the air?" sounds like a value-free question. On the other hand, "Should this stuff be in the air?" appears political. But the first question is as political as the second; it just hides its acquiescence to the status quo. The first question is actually "Since this stuff is in the air, am I likely to get sick?" In a perceptive book about the difference between these two kinds of questions, Alan Garfinkle says, "The individualistic question takes the structural conditions as given. In particular it requires that we not question why these structural conditions are what they are but that we limit our questioning to states of affairs consistent with the structure. . . . The theory that accepts social structure as given and seeks only to maneuver within it is not an alternative to moral theories; it is one among them."[18]

Garfinkel points to the difference between asking a structural question like "Why do large numbers of slum dwellers engage in riots?" and asking an individualistic question like "Why did these particular slum dwellers engage in riots?" He argues that if we really want change, we have to ask the first question, not the second. The same reasoning can apply to disease prevention. Consider the difference between asking "Why do large numbers of people continue to smoke cigarettes?" and asking "Why do these particular people continue to smoke?" The first question directs attention to the tobacco culture in which everyone lives: the growing of tobacco, the advertising of cigarettes, the meaning of smoking. The second question directs attention to the psychology and physiology of individual people within that culture. Prevention concerned solely with these individuals conceals an endorsement of the structure. It also—not to lose sight of what really counts here—is simply less effective than prevention that changes the conditions of the tobacco culture.

Besides influencing the kinds of questions that get asked about toxic substances, individualistic ideology supports attempts to denigrate people worried about them. In considering the risk associated with a substance, if the unit of analysis is the individual, the logical question is "What are my chances of being harmed by it?" Let us say that statistics show the toxin could kill one in ten thousand people. Assuming that each person runs an equal risk, as these analyses do, my personal chances of being killed are very slim. So I am not likely to get particularly worried on that score. Were I to do so, my fear could be easily ridiculed. As long as the public discussion about toxins is in terms of individual risks, the passage of strong regulation is unlikely.

In contrast, consider the nature of the questions people ask when the unit of analysis is the society. With nearly 230 million Americans, a substance toxic to 1 in 10,000 could kill some 23,000 people. That is a quite different issue. It is hard to ridicule proposals to regulate or ban a substance that would cause so many predictable deaths.[19] For this reason, media accounts of newly discovered toxins or of environmental disasters frequently treat as political the *form* in which death estimates are expressed. They give two sides—not two different estimates, but two expressions of the same estimate. Reporting on Chernobyl in *Science*, Colin Norman and David Dickson provide an example. Estimates of cancer deaths, they say, "range from a few thousand to more than 100,000 fatalities." But they then go on to say, "Even the most pessimistic projection would raise overall cancer mortality in the western Soviet Union by only 1%."[20]

But precisely because individualistic ideology is so persuasive, people who insist on analyzing the issue in social or structural terms, who keep talking about "the environment" instead of about specific disease agents found in that environment, are vulnerable to caricature. More, they become types. Just as the nineteenth-century proponents of the miasma theory were able to link the contagion theory to authoritarianism, so the contemporary supporters of the lifestyle and germ theories as ways to explain all disease connect the environmental theory to extremism. People who think in holistic terms about toxins are "environmental activists" and "environmental extremists." People who think individualistically, advocating substance-by-substance regulation and the use, say, of protective devices on the job— these earn no particular labels.

I do not want to imply that we have individualistic disease prevention policies only for ideological reasons. Obviously a theory placing major responsibility on broad social factors is an economic threat both to industry and to the government, which depends for its security on the security of the economy. Neither capitalist nor socialist societies could sustain the kinds of drastic upheavals that would follow an all-out pursuit of synthetic chemicals, unhealthy food, and stressful work environments. So Cuba, for example, is in no better position than the United States to ban or restrict thousands of useful but potentially dangerous agricultural and industrial chemicals. Nor is Cuba any more likely to announce that in order to fight chronic diseases, everybody at work should take whatever breaks necessary to avoid stress on the job. In all countries, reluctance to develop nonindividualistic prevention policies is partly explicable in economic terms. In the United States, however, the economic reason gets reinforced by an ideology that conceptually separates the individual from the society and makes the individual primary. An individualistic analysis of social problems seems "natural." To place responsibility for disease prevention on the society, or the collective, seems wrong. It does not fit. The analysis is suspect.

It is hard to imagine precisely what kinds of disease prevention policies we might have were we not so entranced by individualism. But the Cubans might give us ideas. As I said, their policies could be explicable in purely economic terms. Or we can venture that their rejection of individualism really works and that most Cubans actually make little distinction between themselves as individuals and the collective of which they are a part. As I suggested in chapter four, the closest personal experience most of us have to such a conceptualization is our experience as members of families. Certainly the doctrines of individualism, as descriptions either of what is or of what ought to be, have little to do with family life. Even the most dedicated individualist is willing to sacrifice for the good of all, to think more of group than personal benefit, and to cooperate rather than compete, when the group at issue is his or her family. Even the stereotypical nineteenth-century pater familias with all his overbearing authoritarian attitudes toward his wife and children is concerned for their welfare. And when he thinks of himself as "father" and "husband," he thinks of himself not as an individual but as someone *in relation* to and responsible for other people who created him and are created by him. Something like that may be possible in civic society too.

Certainly it is familiar rhetoric. The heads of multinational companies and the presidents of universities not infrequently encourage their employees to think of the company or the university as a family. At best such rhetoric describes a genuine sentiment among most employees that they really have a personal, giving and receiving relationship with everyone else, people who care about them and about whom they care. At worst it is a blunt appeal to cooperate with authority. In times and places where the family analogy is accurate, individualistic doctrines neither explain social reality nor justify self-seeking behavior. They make no sense. Perhaps in Cuba most people really do feel that the society is like a family. Perhaps they see themselves in a dialectical relationship with "society," one in which they are aware of their power to construct it and its simultaneous power to make them what they are. It might be possible to find out through a content analysis of interviews. One clue would be whether they tend to reify society, that is, to give the collective a reality distinct from their own presence in it. "For the essence of individualism," writes Alasdair MacIntyre, "is not so much to emphasize the individual rather than the collective—whether methodologically or morally—as to frame all questions according to an ostensible antithesis between the individual and the collective. Those who continue to base their thinking on this false antithesis even if . . . they champion the claims of the collective against the individual, remain within the basic categories of individualist thought and practice."[21]

Nonindividualistic disease prevention policies, then, would recognize a dialectical relation between the individual and the collective, empowering people to take charge of their lives by giving them legitimate power over the conditions in which they live and work. The responsibility to exercise, eat healthful foods, use personal protective devices at work, and stop smoking would occur within a context where people also had genuine power to change the environment. They could design a workday that made time and place for exercise; they could help determine what foods would be available; they could influence decisions about the use of toxic substances; they could create policies for the production, distribution, and consumption of cigarettes.

Unfortunately, however, more than an individualistic ideology stands in the way of participatory and effective disease prevention policies. A belief central to science constitutes another barrier.

SCIENCE

Like individualism, science is both a collection of ideological beliefs and an agency for liberation. As an agency for liberation it substitutes democracy for political and religious authority. Demanding evidence for statements of fact and providing criteria to test the evidence, it gives us a way to distinguish between what is true and what powerful people might wish to convince us is true. In addition its discoveries in medicine and technology have reduced infectious disease, increased communication, improved transportation, made work less exhausting, provided more leisure time, and enriched diets. Only in the last forty years have large numbers of people begun to recognize the negative corollaries of scientific achievements. But these, including the stultifying alienation for many people from their work, the increasing dispersal of toxic substances into the environment, and the unimaginably destructive instruments of war, are not inevitable consequences of scientific progress. Instead they largely result from accepting science's central dogma: reality can only be accurately investigated by rigorously separating the objective from the subjective.

The identification of "true" knowledge with objective knowledge is part of a general dualistic world view in which mind and body, fact and value, reason and emotion, and so on are polar opposites. The concept supports the view that nature exists independently of scientists' attempts to study it and that scientists discover nature's truths by bracketing off their own values and emotions. However at odds with our new understanding of what scientists actually do, the idea strikes a responsive chord, not only because it makes science dependable, but because it is consistent with individualism. Lukes points out that individualism's praise of personal autonomy, taken to its logical conclusion, locates the source of all morality in the individual. If man is autonomous, he asks, "why should not the very choice of values, of the criteria of evaluation, be up to him?" From this follows a moral relativism in which "no empirical description of the world compels us to adopt any particular set of moral evaluations or principles, or even limits to the range of our possible values and preferences."[22] Facts are in one category, values in another.

Dualism has philosophical roots in the seventeenth century, beginning with Descarte's proposal that nature is analytically comparable to a machine. Like a machine, it has separate parts, he postulated, operating in concert with one another in a regular and lawlike way. The machine model of nature had a certain usefulness, but when the model was extended to humans, something was clearly left out. There was no room for the nonempirical aspects of humans: their minds, their souls, or their consciousness. So as R. C. Lewontin, Steven Rose, and Leon Kamin observe, "there had to be two sorts of stuff in nature: matter, subject to the mechanical laws of physics; and soul or mind. . . . So developed the inevitable but fatal disjunction of Western scientific thought. . . . [S]ome sort of dualism is the inevitable consequence of any sort of reductionist materialism that does not in the end wish to accept that humans are 'nothing but' the motion of their molecules."[23]

Both the reductionism inherent in the machine model and the dualism it generates lead to narrow analyses of disease causality and limited proposals for prevention policy. In the first place, like the ideology of individualism, the ideology in science takes for granted a reductionist unit of analysis. Hence, it reinforces the political assumptions that impugn structural analyses of causality. Even when much demographic data and historical research indicate that disease is a consequence of poverty, the search for the causes of illnesses readily gets reduced to the identification of toxic agents. If no agents can be identified, analysis moves to personal behavior, frequently studied in isolation from its social context, as in the air traffic control case. Within this reality, research that takes the social structure as the unit of analysis gets pushed to the periphery of science. At most it is a lesser kind of science—social science. At worst it is not science at all but a pseudoscience contaminated with politics. Thus the analyses most likely to result in prevention policies with the most impact on health are least likely to earn the label "science."

Such thinking is no respecter of political culture. In 1983 the Chinese began a new long-term study, sponsored by the World Health Organization, to see whether a vaccine can prevent hepatocellular carcinoma. Earlier epidemiologic research showed that many people with hepatocellular carcinoma, a rapidly fatal liver cancer, had also had, as much as twenty to thirty years previously, hepatitis B virus (HBV) infections. The new study, using vaccine effective both against HBV and chronic liver disease, is documenting the vaccine's long-term effect on liver cancer rates. All this seems unremarkable unless you know that HBV is spread largely through poor sanitation. Indeed, in the United States, HBV is rare precisely because we have better sanitation and hygiene than China.[24] This information returns us to familiar ground. A reductionist analysis of disease leads the Chinese to search for a cause of cancer in a virus. Evidence collected from a more structural perspective points to poor sanitation. The hidden assumption in the reductionist view is that distributing vaccine is preferable (economically? politically?) to providing good sanitation. One can imagine in China eventual health education posters urging people to get their HBV shots and earnest discussions among health professionals about how to motivate people to attend clinics. All this could be avoided by improved sanitation, just as it is in the United States.

So, like individualism, science encourages reductionist concepts of disease. But science also encourages dualism; and dualism, like reductionism, has a bias of its own. As we have seen, a dualistic ideology sets up two logical categories of knowledge: objective and subjective. The objective category presumes to exclude personal values and political preferences. People speaking and writing in the objective mode try to strip their language of words and phrases that would call attention to the existence of an actual person behind them, lest the knowledge they impart seem nonprofessional, contaminated by human agency, and thus neither scientific nor neutral. The practice, however, can hide political judgments.

"Not statistically significant" means, according to the author of a current medical statistics textbook, that the data "fail to provide sufficient evidence to doubt the validity of the null hypothesis." (Translation: "Not statistically significant" means we do not have enough data yet.) He continues: "'Not significant' indicates that one has to live with the null hypothesis value until other evidence is obtained."[25] This sterile phraseology, besides teaching medical students to use mystifying language, avoids acknowledging that "live with the null hypothesis" means "live with" a suspected cause of disease. The bland language hides the grim authoritarian voice. It implies that what "one" lives with is merely a hypothesis. Suppose the author had written "When our studies don't show anything yet, they indicate that people have to live with a suspected toxic substance." Certainly a reasonable response from the people in question might be "Why? Who says that an absence of data means we have to take risks?" You cannot answer the questions and pretend that no one is making any choices here. At least without the passive voice and arcane terminology, it is hard to sustain the position that condoning people's exposure to a possible hazard is a neutral act.

More than simply hiding political judgments in aseptic language, the radical distinction between objective and subjective knowledge favors certain kinds of political judgments. It biases science toward protecting the status quo. For example, when toxicologic or epidemiologic information is incomplete or contested, to state that until scientists are sure, people should be protected is apparently to speak ethically, not scientifically. It is to speak on matters of right and wrong, which the dualistic presupposition takes to be subjective, not on matters of true and false, which dualism takes to be objective. So scientists who speak publicly in favor of protecting people even when (or because) the data are unclear or contested become vulnerable to the charge of bias. But ethical matters are *built in* to scientific matters. A refusal to speak out can have as many health consequences as a willingness to do so. If a possible toxic substance contaminates the water or air, it is not a neutral act to leave it there. The scientist who knows that a substance may be harmful but hesitates to advocate a protection policy acts on matters of principle just as does the scientist who publicly supports protection. But the silent scientist is justified for his or her lack of action because the silence is consistent with the belief in a natural distinction between the subjective and the objective, and between ethics and science. Elizabeth Fee makes just this point:

> The voices of scientific authority are more often called upon to quiet public distress than to articulate the grounds for concern; scientific expertise becomes a shield against the effort to ensure public accountability. In this context, scientists who retreat behind the screen of pure science are passively abandoning their social responsibility; those who choose to become actively involved risk being seen no longer "objective". Here the notion of "objectivity" becomes merely a code word for the political passivity of those scientists who have tacitly agreed to accept a privileged social position and freedom of inquiry within the laboratory in return for their silence in not questioning the social uses of science or the power relations which determine its direction.[26]

The same reasoning characterizes the social sciences. To blur the distinction between objective and subjective knowledge in the study of the social world risks one's claim to the title "scientist." Thus many social scientists shrink from social criticism. Except, as Barrington Moore points out,

> at the technical level of asserting that certain means are unlikely to bring about the desired results, i.e., concentration camps may not be the most efficient way to eliminate the Jews. If the purpose of the state is eliminating Jews, there is nothing more to be said

from this conception. . . . The goals of the state are, for the political scientist, brute facts to be entered in his calculations the way a physicist enters gravity, friction, and the character of metals in his computations. According to this viewpoint, the moment the political scientist steps out of his professional role to assert that killing Jews is morally bad, he enters the realm of "values", loses his aura of professional competence, and becomes no more qualified to give authoritative guidance than any of the rest of us.[27]

IMPLICATIONS

Not until well into the twentieth century was the reality of dualisms seriously questioned. Today, however, a provocative and growing literature displays a new conviction that the dualistic concepts so deeply etched in the modern mind are ideologies. As we saw in chapter six, contemporary philosophers argue that theory and observation are inevitably and inextricably entangled. Instead of being able to stand apart from the world and look at it dispassionately, scientists, like everyone else, necessarily bring to the observation presuppositions, values, and emotions. This rejection of the very categories of thought that once distinguished modern from traditional cultures has opened the possibility of new, richer methods. It has challenged the distinction between science and the humanities and has created a postmodern sensibility in which the familiar "objective," "scientific" descriptions of reality seem sterile, thin, and limited. Instead of confining their research to "facts" that can be known empirically, postmodernists look also for the meaning those facts have in the contexts in which they appear. In one way or another, the new methodologies aim at describing the social construction of reality.

But is there not a problem here? If we insist that the mind and the body, the subjective and the objective, are not separable, then we seemingly have no grounds on which to accept or reject any particular proposition about the cause of disease beyond political preferences. If we say that there are no facts unmediated by values, we apparently have to agree with the Tobacco Institute and the Mobile Oil Company that the toxicity of cigarettes or synthetic chemicals is just a matter of interpretation. If we question the ability of science to settle policy arguments, we seemingly have no way methodically to test and refute xenophobic, superstitious, bigoted, or thoughtless beliefs. For example, we cannot find out whether graphic depictions of sexual violence are causally related to rape, whether teenagers get pregnant because they do not know about contraception, whether advertising is an important influence on smoking, or whether dioxin makes people sick. If we cannot depend on scientific methodology to discover facts, we are ostensibly at the mercy of whoever has the political power to make his or her views predominate.

And this is the dilemma. As liberating as postmodernism can be, it risks a radical relativism. Concentrating on what things *mean*, it skirts the question of what things *are*. Postmodern philosophy recognizes that what we know is mediated by who we are. There is no pristine observation; we are always a level removed from actual reality. Given this recognition, the practitioners of the new perspective study the mediator. They examine the text, not the thing it describes; the signifier, not the signified; the representation, not the represented. Since the subjective is so intertwined with the objective, they seem to say, no one can know anything for sure. In the final analysis, there is no reality, only different perceptions.

Surely there is something wrong with that conclusion. Intellectuals can talk themselves into accepting it theoretically, but who actually *lives* as though reality is not knowable? There lies insanity. A preoccupation with the social construction of reality easily becomes a mere intellectual game. Take the case of sexuality. As Carole Vance has pointed out, you can do elegant and entertaining studies of the meaning it has in different societies, the various rules people devise about its expression, the historical development of particular classifications of sexuality (the category of homosexual did not exist until recent times, for example) and the way that sexual desire acquires significance in specific cultural contexts. But if sexuality is entirely socially constructed, then, in some sense, the body does not even exist. Both sexuality and desire become trivial.[28] Leslie Rado has made a similar argument about cultural studies of the body. Behind all the discourse about the body's meaning, there exists a *real thing* complete with blood, intestines, and brain matter. It includes the capacity for pain, and the eventuality of death. Understanding how the body is mediated by culture and society is important, but to lose touch, so to speak, with the real thing can alienate us from ourselves, from our bodies, and thus from one another.[29] In the same vein, the questions I have been raising about the meanings causal statements acquire, about whether scientists speak out or not, and about who is supposed to take risks would be of little real consequence if, regardless of what happens, no one would get sick. Postmodern philosophy with all its emphasis on interpretation implies that we have to deny our quest—the dramatic cliché *is* appropriate—for truth.

The postmodern conclusion that there is no reality, only different perceptions, misses the point. It takes for granted the very dualisms it claims to challenge, for it assumes that values are indeed the opposite of facts. The only reason one would, however, throw out facts, on the basis that they include values, would be if one believed that values are entirely personal and subjective and that it is impossible to discriminate among them. It would be more logical to assume that, just as values hide within facts, so facts hide within values. Stephen Toulmin seems prepared to make such an argument when he says, "It might have been better if philosophers and scientists had emphasized the similarities between science and ethics, and had used the 'rational objectivity' of science as a model in seeking to reestablish the claims of moral objectivity as well. The argument that ethical issues are, in their own proper ways, as public and intersubjective as scientific issues (and so equally 'rational') was . . . abandoned too quickly and lightly."[30]

We can address in two ways the fear that including values threatens facts. One is by considering dialectics, and the other is by taking another look at values."Dialectics" sounds like jargon. Only academics employ the word, and they are usually vague about what it means. I hesitate to use it at all, except that no other term adequately conveys, either, what I want to address: a way of thinking to substitute for dualism that still leaves us with some claim to be able to know reality. It is no wonder that we have no handy word; we have no handy concept. "Modern" people are all dualists. The closest we usually get to a dialectical vision is to recognize that things can interact to form new entities unlike their constituent parts. Hydrogen and oxygen, for example, are gasses; but together they form water, with qualities of wetness and temperature. This understanding, though, does not address the relation of apparent opposites, and it is essentially static. A dialectical view is more complex than this. It imagines component parts in continual interaction. It holds that mind and body, for example, create one another; they are never entirely one thing or the other. In the same way, the individual and society are not reducible to one antipode or the other. Rather than being distinct parts, they are wholes in process. Being and becoming simultaneously. At every level of explanation, down to the molecular, all we have is interaction. We never arrive at a static, fixed base.

Reviewing two books by a British organization called the Dialectics of Biology Group, R. C. Lewontin writes, "What characterizes dialectics is the rejection of the terms of the argument that places all questions somewhere on a line between explanations by properties of parts and explanations by emergent properties of wholes. It is not that a whole is more than the sum of its parts, but that the parts themselves are re-defined and re-created in the process of their interaction."[31] In a book of his own, Lewontin, a geneticist, joins a neurobiologist and a psychologist in arguing against reductionist explanations: "We must insist that a full understanding of the human condition demands an integration of the biological and the social in which neither is given primacy or ontological priority over the other but in which they are seen as being related in a dialectical manner, a manner that distinguishes epistemologically between levels of explanation relating to the social without collapsing one into the other or denying the existence of either."[32]

Dialectical reasoning would make a similar case for facts and values. It would continue on from the description of values' influence on facts to one of facts' influence on values. At the very least, it would resist the utilitarian notion that a right action is only knowable by its consequences. It would reject the related position that all ethical arguments for and against a policy are equal. It would deny that there is no way to distinguish between good and bad arguments because it would conceive of values existing in interaction with facts, not as separate realities with no connection to an external, objective world.

The second way to address the fear of admitting values into facts is to take another look at values. Here I turn for inspiration to Sandra Harding. In *The Science Question in Feminism* she argues, as have many before her, that science is shot through with values.[33] What distinguishes her work (along with that of other feminists) from earlier philosophers like Kuhn is that she thinks the values are terrible. Harding argues that when the dominant political ideology is racist, sexist, classist, and imperialist, these assumptions will necessarily permeate scientific research that tries to be neutral. If no methodology can eliminate values from science, then scientists should be guided not by unconscious racism and so on but by "participatory values—antiracism, anti-classism, antisexism—that decrease the distortions and mystifications in our culture's explanations and understandings."[34] Like Lewontin and his colleagues, Harding is looking for a methodology that will yield the most accurate description of reality; like them, she wants to retain the possibility of a scientific knowledge. But she is less concerned with describing the dialectical interaction of biology and society. For her, the fundamental issue is what kind of society interacts, because, she argues, some moral and political beliefs admit an accurate description of reality, while others distort it. She concludes that "the paradigm models of objective science are those studies explicitly directed by morally and politically emancipatory interests—that is, by interests in eliminating sexist, racist, classist, and culturally coercive understandings of nature and social life."[35]

To apply this reasoning to the question of disease causality, if we want prevention policies that really work because they protect most people, then scientists have to incorporate egalitarian values in their search for truth. Truth, after all, is a goal; like justice and democracy, it is ellusive and challengeable. We may never actually reach it. New information and different moral and political beliefs transfigure old truths, forcing us to begin the search again. But the instability of truth is not lamentable. It springs from the vitality of the world and the passions of people, their struggles to understand, their visions of perfection. The reality that truth is only discoverable by human beings, in all their humanness, does not mean that we must abandon the hope of finding it. We just have to hold facts lightly, continually testing them against experience and logic, recognizing their connection to the rules and contexts within which they appear, and most important, never ceasing to scrutinize the values that necessarily permeate them.

In other words, we do not have to choose between a desire to find the "real" causes of disease and an acceptance of the connection between facts and values. Instead, before we ask after the cause of disease, we must ask what values should guide the search. Values are public issues. Given that people who subscribe to the ideologies of individualism and positivism will probably make reductionistic analyses and come up with individualistic policies, and given that these are usually less effective than broad analyses and socially based policies, we need public discussion about the values, beliefs, and ideologies with which scientists and policy makers begin. This is not an unwarranted intrusion of politics into science. There is no science uninfluenced by politics. This is a plea to get the politics out of hiding.

Notes

Chapter One: Nineteenth-Century Debates

1. Michael W. Flinn, Introduction, in Edwin Chadwick, *The Report on the Sanitary Condition of the Labouring Population of Great Britain* (1842; reprint, Edinburgh: Edinburgh University Press, 1965), 11.

2. Thomas McKeown, *The Modern Rise of Population* (New York: Academic, 1976).

3. William Hobson, *World Health and History* (Bristol: Wright, 1963); Hanz Zinsser, *Rats, Lice and History* (Boston: Little, Brown, 1935).

4. Flinn, in Chadwick, *Sanitary Condition*, 10.

5. Ibid., 13.

6. Roderick McGrew, *Russia and the Cholera 1823–1932* (Madison: University of Wisconsin Press, 1965), 91.

7. Charles Creighton, *A History of Epidemics in Britain*, vol. 2 (1894; reprint, London: Cass, 1965), 815.

8. Ibid., 821.

9. Erwin H. Ackerknecht, *History and Geography of the Most Important Diseases* (New York: Hafner, 1965), 26.

10. Geoffrey Marks and William K. Beatty, *Epidemics* (New York: Scribner's, 1976), 250.

11. Creighton, *History of Epidemics*, 140.

12. Marks and Beatty, *Epidemics*, 253.

13. Charles-Edward Amory Winslow, *The Conquest of Epidemic Disease: A Chapter in the History of Ideas* (Madison: University of Wisconsin Press, 1980), 193.

179

14. George Rosen, *A History of Public Health* (New York: MD Publications, 1958), 234.

15. Ibid., 68.

16. McGrew, *Russia and the Cholera*, 48.

17. John Harvey Powell, *Bring Out Your Dead: The Great Plague of Yellow Fever in Philadelphia in 1793* (Philadelphia: University of Pennsylvania Press, 1949), 223.

18. McGrew, *Russia and the Cholera*, 78.

19. Ibid., 46; John Duffy, *Sword of Pestilence: The New Orleans Yellow Fever Epidemic of 1853* (Baton Rouge: Louisiana State University Press, 1966), 45.

20. McGrew, *Russia and the Cholera*, 109–110.

21. Shakespeare Association, *Present Remedies against the Plague, etc.*, facsimile of the 1603 ed. (London: Oxford University Press, 1933), ix.

22. McGrew, *Russia and the Cholera*, 46.

23. Hobson, *World Health and History*, 81.

24. Powell, *Bring Out Your Dead*, 46.

25. Quoted in Marks and Beatty, *Epidemics*, 80.

26. Quoted in John C. Gunn, *Gunn's New Family Physician: or, Home Book of Health* (Cincinnati: Wilstach, Baldwin, 1883), 417.

27. Philip Ziegler, *The Black Death* (New York: John Day, 1969), 103.

28. Ibid., 961; Ackerknecht, *History and Geography*, 14.

29. Odair Franco, "The First Yellow Fever Epidemic in Brazil," in *A Febre Amarela no Seculo XVIII no Brasil*, Ministry of Health publication (Rio de Janeiro: Blücher, 1971), 89–99.

30. McGrew, *Russia and the Cholera*, 7, 110, 130.

31. Even Engels thought the Irish were uncivilized savages. See Frederick Engels, "The Condition of the Working Class in England," in *Kark Marx, Frederick Engels: Collected Works* (New York: International Publishers, 1975), 4:389–392.

32. Ilza Veith, "Plague Politics," *Bulletin of the History of Medicine* 28 (1954): 408–416.

33. Erwin H. Ackerknecht, "Anticontagionism between 1821 and 1967," *Bulletin of the History of Medicine* 22 (1948): 563.

34. Eric J. Hobsbawn, *The Age of Revolution 1789–1848* (New York: New American Library, 1964), 57.

35. Ibid., 53.

36. S. G. Checkland, *The Rise of Industrial Society in England 1815–1885* (New York: St. Martin's, 1964), 37–38.

37. Ackerknecht, "Anticontagionism."

38. Ibid., 590–591.

39. John Wesley, *Primitive Physick: or, An Easy and Natural Method of Curing Most Diseases* (1749; reprint, London: G. Woodfall, n.d.), 111.

40. John Ballard Blake, *Public Health in the Town of Boston 1630–1822* (Cambridge: Harvard University Press, 1959).

41. Duffy, *Sword of Pestilence*, 90; Charles E. Rosenberg, *The Cholera Years: The United States in 1832, 1849, and 1866* (Chicago: University of Chicago Press, 1962), 47–48.

42. McGrew, *Russia and the Cholera*, 111.

43. Quoted in Duffy, *Sword of Pestilence*, 91.

44. Quoted in Rosenberg, *Cholera Years*, 43.

45. Quoted in ibid., 44.

46. Martin S. Pernick, "Politics, Parties and Pestilence: Epidemic Yellow Fever in Philadelphia and the Rise of the First Party System," in *Sickness and Health in America: Readings in the History of Medicine and Public Health*, ed. Judith Waltzer Leavitt and Ronald L. Numbers (Madison: University of Wisconsin Press, 1985), 360.

47. Rosenberg, *Cholera Years*.

48. Arthur M. Schlesinger, Jr., *The Age of Jackson* (Boston: Little, Brown, 1946).

49. Carl Russell Fish, *The Rise of Common Man 1830–1850* (New York: Macmillan, 1927), 12.

50. Quoted in ibid., 268.

51. John B. Boles, *The Great Revival 1787–1805* (Lexington: University Press of Kentucky, 1972).

52. Quoted in Charles C. Cole, *The Social Ideas of the Northern Evangelists 1826–1860.* (New York: Octagon, 1966), 138.

53. Richard Harrison Shryock, *Medicine in America: Historical Essays* (Baltimore: John Hopkins Press, 1966).

54. Russel Blaine Nye, *Society and Culture in America 1830–1860* (New York: Harper & Row, 1974).

55. Ibid.; Ronald L. Numbers, "Do-It-Yourself the Sectarian Way," in *Medicine without Doctors*, ed. Guenther B. Risse, Ronald L. Numbers, and Judith Walzer Leavitt (New York: Watson Academic, Science History Publications, 1977), 49–72.

56. Shryock, *Medicine in America*; Nye, *Society and Culture*; John Duffy, *The Healers: The Rise of the Medical Establishment* (New York: McGraw-Hill, 1976); Harry B. Weiss and Howard R. Kemble, *They Took to the Waters: The Forgotten Mineral Spring Resorts of New Jersey and Nearby Pennsylvania and Delaware* (Norwalk, Conn.: Gibson, Pastime Press,

1962); Samuel Levy Bensusan, *Some German Spas: A Holiday Record* (London: Douglas, 1925).

57. Noah Webster, *A Brief History of Epidemic and Pestilential Disease with the Principal Phenomena of the Physical World Which Precede and Accompany Them and Observation Deduced from the Facts Stated*, vol. 2 (1799; reprint, New York: Burt Franklin, 1970), 232.

58. Ibid., 233.
59. Ibid., 234.
60. Ibid., 235.
61. Ibid., 238.
62. Gunn, *Gunn's New Family Physician*, 183.
63. Hippocrates, "Airs Waters and Places," in *The Genuine Works of Hippocrates*, trans. Francis Adams (New York: William Wood, 1886), 156.
64. Thomas Sydenham, *The Whole Works of That Excellent Practical Physician Dr. Thomas Sydenham*, 2d ed. corrected from the original Latin by John Pechey (London: R. Wellington, 1697), 5.
65. Charles-Edward Amory Winslow, *The Conquest of Epidemic Diseases* (Princeton, N.J.: Princeton University Press, 1943), 66.
66. Duffy, *Sword of Pestilence*, 87–88.
67. Franco, "Yellow Fever," 92.
68. Powell, *Bring Out Your Dead*, 46.
69. Quoted in Samuel E. Finer, *The Life and Times of Sir Edwin Chadwick* (London: Methuen, 1952), 297.
70. Ibid., 215.
71. Edwin Chadwick, *Sanitary Condition*, 91–92.
72. Ibid., 104–105.
73. Ibid., 108.
74. Ibid., 135–150.
75. Ibid., 396–410, 423–425.
76. Rosen, *History of Public Health*, 224.
77. Finer, *Sir Edwin Chadwick*; Flinn, Introduction, in Chadwick, *Sanitary Condition*.
78. Chadwick, *Sanitary Condition*, 167.
79. Ibid., 167.
80. Ibid., 256.
81. Ibid., 256.
82. Ibid., 254.
83. Ibid., 423.
84. Ibid., 325.

Chapter Two: Twentieth-Century Debates

1. Department of Health and Human Services (DHHS), *Health: United States 1985*, Public Health Service Publication no. 86–1232, table 16, p. 46.

2. Evelyn M. Kitagawa and Philip M. Hauser, *Differential Mortality in the United States* (Cambridge: Harvard University Press, 1973); M. G. Marmot, M. J. Shipley, and Geoffrey Rose, "Inequalities in Death: Specific Explanation of a General Pattern?" *Lancet*, 5 May 1984; 1003–1006; Constantine A. Yeracaris, "Socioeconomic Differentials in Selected Causes of Death," *American Journal of Public Health* 68 (1978): 342–351; Great Britain, Office of Population Censuses and Surveys, *Occupational Mortality*, the Registrar General's Decennial Supplement for England and Wales, 1970–1972, ser. DS, no. 1 (London: HMSO, 1978); DHHS, *Report of the Secretary's Task Force on Black and Minority Health*, Washington, D.C., 16 Oct. 1985. For a synopsis of the latter report, see the *Morbidity and Mortality Weekly Report*, 28 Feb. 1986.

3. Aaron Antonovsky, "Social Class, Life Expectancy, and Overall Mortality," *Milbank Memorial Fund Quarterly* 45(1967): 31–73.

4. See especially Alastair McIntosh Gray, "Inequalities in Health. The Black Report: A Summary and Comment," *International Journal of Health Services* 12(1982): 349–380. Note also that in England, the Working Group on Inequalities in Health, established by the Secretary of State for Social Services in 1977, said in its 1980 report that, despite the existence of the National Health Service, inequality in health had not diminished and was probably increasing. See U.K., Department of Health and Social Security, *Inequalities in Health: Report of a Research Working Group* (1980), Foreword by Patrick Jenkin, Secretary of State for Social Services.

5. John Cairns, *Cancer: Science and Society* (San Francisco: W. H. Freeman, 1978), 115.

6. The isolation of HTLV III, the AIDS virus, is changing this opinion to some extent. See Jean L. Marx, "The Slow, Insidious Natures of the HTLVs," *Science* 231 (1986): 450–541. But also see G. J. Todaro, "Summary: Tumor Virus Genes in the 'Real World'—Current Status," in *Viruses in Naturally Occurring Cancers*, ed. Myron Essex, George J. Todaro, and Harold zur Hausen, Cold Springs Harbor (N.Y.) Conferences on Cell Proliferation, 1980, 7:1259–1274.

7. Robert Gallo, "The Virus-Cancer Story," *Hospital Practice* (June

1983): 79–89; Roger Lewin, "New Reports of a Human Leukemia Virus," *Science* 214(1981): 530–531; "Tumor Viruses," unsigned editorial, *Lancet*, 6 Feb. 1982; 317–318.

8. Richard Doll, "Introduction," in *Origins of Human Cancer*, ed. H. H. Hiatt, J. D. Watson, and J. A. Winsten, Cold Springs Harbor (N.Y.) Conferences on Cell Proliferation, 1977, 4:1–12; *Lancet*, 6 Feb. 1982; 317–318; Todaro, "Summary."

9. Thomas McKeown, *The Modern Rise of Population* (New York: Academic, 1976).

10. People who nevertheless answer "germs" when asked about the causes of disease can be excused for a lack of historical perspective but not for blindness to the narrow applicability of the theory. Microorganisms have been implicated only in a few diseases; scores of other ailments fall outside the scope of the germ theory. Consider the following list of diagnostic terms: hypertension, asthma, senility, malnutrition, alcoholism, hemophilia, concussion, emphysema, muscular dystrophy, lead poisoning, duodenal ulcer, gallstones, multiple sclerosis, coronary thrombosis, diabetes, and cirrhosis of the liver.

11. This is a favorite theme in Lewis Thomas's "Notes of a Biology Watcher" column in the *New England Journal of Medicine*. For his remarks on science in general, see ibid., 296(1977): 324–328. For his entertaining criticism of the lifestyle theory of disease causality, see ibid., 299(1978): 461–463.

12. For discussions of this point, see Howard Berliner and J. Warren Salmon, "The Holistic Alternative to Scientific Medicine: History and Analysis," *International Journal of Health Services* 10(1980): 133–147; Meredith Turshen, "The Political Ecology of Disease," *Review of Radical Political Economics* 9(Spring 1977): 45–60.

13. Department of Health, Education and Welfare (DHEW), *Healthy People: The Surgeon General's Report on Health Promotion and Disease Prevention 1979*, Public Health Service Publication no. 79-55071.

14. Arthur Upton, testimony at hearings before the Subcommittee on Nutrition of the Senate Committee on Agriculture, Nutrition, and Forestry, 12–13 June 1978.

15. *New York Times*, 17 June 1982.

16. Ibid., 29 Sept. 1983; ibid., 13 Dec. 1984.

17. N. Fiore, "Fighting Cancer: One Patient's Perspective," *New England Journal of Medicine* 300(1979): 284–289.

18. Gavin Andrews, Christopher Tennant, Daphne Hewson, and Malcolm Schonell, "The Relation of Social Factors to Physical and Psychiatric Illness," *American Journal of Epidemiology* 108(July 1978): 27–35.

19. Jean Tache, Hans Selye, and Stacey Day, eds., *Cancer, Stress, and Death* (New York: Plenum, 1979), 14.

20. Nancy Harman Jenkins, "A New Benefit in the Workplace Is Spreading Good Nutrition," *New York Times*, 27 Nov. 1985; R. Cunningham, *Wellness at Work: A Report on Health and Fitness Programs for Employees of Business and Industry* (Chicago: Blue Cross Association, 1982).

21. DHHS, Office on Smoking and Health, *The Health Consequences of Smoking: Cancer*, a report of the Surgeon General, 1982.

22. DHHS, Office on Smoking and Health, *The Health Consequences of Smoking: Cardiovascular Disease*, a report of the Surgeon General, 1983.

23. Walter C. Willett and Brian MacMahon, "Diet and Cancer: An Overview," *New England Journal of Medicine* 310(1984): 633–638.

24. Gina Kolata, "Heart Panel's Conclusions Questioned," *Science* 227 (1985): 40–41.

25. Eliot Marshall, "The Academy Kills a Nutrition Report," *Science* 230(1985): 420–421.

26. Willet and MacMahon, "Diet and Cancer"; see also Victor Herbert, Letter to *Science* 233(1986): 926.

27. Willet and MacMahon, "Diet and Cancer."

28. Gina Kolata, "Value of Low Sodium Diets Questioned," *Science* 216(1982): 38–39.

29. Eliot Marshall, "Diet Advice, with a Grain of Salt and a Large Helping of Pepper," *Science* 231(1986): 537–539.

30. Willett and MacMahon, "Diet and Cancer."

31. George V. Mann, "Diet-Heart: End of an Era," *New England Journal of Medicine* 297(1977): 644.

32. DHEW, *Healthy People*, 135.

33. See chap. 5, this volume.

34. DHEW, *Healthy People*, 133. For a more recent report from the Harvard study, see Ralph Paffenbarger, Robert T. Hyde, Alvin L. Wing, and Chung-Cheng Hsiah, "Physical Activity, All-Cause Mortality, and Longevity in College Alumni," *New England Journal of Medicine* 314(1986): 605–613.

35. Muriel R. Gillick, "Health Promotion, Jogging, and the Pursuit of the Moral Life," *Journal of Health Politics, Policy, and Law* 9(Fall 1984): 369–387. See also *Public Health Reports* 100(Mar.–Apr. 1985); the entire issue is devoted to physical activity.

36. Samuel S. Epstein and Joel B. Swartz, Letter to *Science* 224 (1984): 660–666.

37. Nathan J. Karch and Marvin A. Schneiderman, "Explaining the

Urban Factor in Lung Cancer Mortality," Congress, House Committee on Energy and Commerce, Subcommittee on Health and the Environment, *Clean Air Act (Part 2)*, 97th Cong., 1st sess., 16 Dec., 1981, Serial 97-103, 491–572. Devra Lee Davis, Kenneth Bridbord, and Marvin Schneiderman, "Cancer Prevention: Assessing Causes, Exposure, and Recent Trends in Mortality for U.S. Males, 1968–1978," *International Journal of Health Services* 13(1983): 337–368; Samuel S. Epstein and Joel B. Swartz, "Fallacies in Lifestyle Cancer Theories," *Nature* 289 (1981): 127–130; T. D. Sterling, "Filtering Information about Occupation, Smoking, and Disease," *Journal of Chronic Diseases* 37(1984): 227–230; idem, "Does Smoking Kill Workers or Working Kill Smokers?" *International Journal of Health Services* 8(1978): 437–452.

38. Robert Crawford, "You Are Dangerous to Your Health: The Ideology and Politics of Victim Blaming," *International Journal of Health Services* 7(1977): 663–680.

39. Marc Lalonde, *A New Perspective on the Health of Canadians: A Working Document* (Ottawa, 1974). For comments see E. Vayda, "Keeping People Well: A New Approach to Medicine," *Human Nature* 1(July 1978): 64–71.

40. B. Stokes, "Self Care: A Nation's Best Health Insurance," *Science* 205(1979): 64–71.

41. Howard Berliner, "Emerging Ideologies in Medicine," *Review of Radical Political Economics* 9(Spring 1977): 116–124.

42. Leon Eisenberg, "The Perils of Prevention: A Cautionary Note," *New England Journal of Medicine* 297(1977): 1231.

43. Epstein and Swartz, "Fallacies"; Davis, "Cancer Prevention."

44. Anthony Robbins, director of the National Institute of Occupational Safety and Health, in a statement to the House Subcommittee on Labor Standards of the Committee on Education and Labor Hearings, May 1, 2, and 8, 1979.

45. William J. Nicolson, George Perkel, and Irving J. Selikoff, "Occupational Exposure to Asbestos: Population at Risk and Projected Mortality—1980–2030," *American Journal of Industrial Medicine* 3(1982): 259–311.

46. *HEW Physician Advisory Bulletin*, 25 Apr. 1978.

47. DHHS, Public Health Service, *Promoting Health/Preventing Illness: Objectives for the Nation*, Fall 1980, 40.

48. Office of Technology Assessment, *Preventing Illness and Injury in the Workplace*, OTA-H-256, Apr. 1985, 43.

49. *Toxicity Testing: Strategies to Determine Needs and Priorities* (Washington, D.C.: National Academy Press, 1984).

50. Barbara Culleton, "Toxic Substances Legislation: How Well Are Laws Being Implemented?" *Science* 201(1978): 1198–1199.

51. R. H. Harris, T. Page, and N. A. Reiches, "Carcinogenic Hazards of Organic Chemicals in Drinking Water," in *Origins of Human Cancer*, ed. H. H. Hiatt, J. D. Watson, and J. A. Winsten, Cold Springs Harbor (N.Y.) Conferences on Cell Proliferation, 1977, 5:309–330.

52. Office of Technology Assessment, *Protecting the Nation's Groundwater from Contamination*, OTA-O-233, Oct. 1984, 1:63.

53. *New York Times*, 20 May 1985; see also *New York Times*, 26 Mar. 1985, for a longer report on this survey conducted by the House Subcommittee on Health and Environment.

54. Robert Hoover, "Investigations of Geographic Variation in Cancer Mortality within the USA," *Cancer Epidemiology in the USA and USSR*, DHHS, National Institutes of Health Publication No. 80-2044, July 1980.

55. R. J. Smith, "Toxic Substances: EPA and OSHA Are Reluctant Regulators," *Science* 203(1979): 28–32.

56. *Critical Mass Journal* 5 (Jan. 1980): unpaged.

57. In an interview with the *New York Times*, John W. Gofman, professor emeritus of medical physics at the University of California, said, "In the next thirty years medicine is going to sign about 1,400,000 death warrants as a result of unnecessary [diagnostic] radiation exposure." *New York Times*, 2 Sept. 1982. For additional reports on radiation, see Karl Z. Morgan, "Cancer and Low Level Radiation," *Bulletin of Atomic Scientists* 34(1978): 30–40, and Congress, House Committee on Interstate and Foreign Commerce, Subcommittee on Health and the Environment, *Effect of Radiation on Human Health: Health Effects of Ionizing Radiation*. 95th Cong., 2d sess., 24–26 Jan., 8, 9, 14, 28 Feb., 1978, Serial 95-179.

58. Genevieve M. Matanoski, "Risk of Cancer Associated with Occupational Exposure in Radiologists and Other Radiation Workers," in *Cancer: Achievements, Challenges and Prospects for the 1980s*, ed. J. H. Burchenal and H. F. Oettgen (New York: Grune & Stratton, 1980), 1:241–254.

59. The 90 percent figure comes from Congress, Senate Committee on Environment and Public Works, *Health Effects of Toxic Pollution: A Report from the Surgeon General*, 96th Cong., 2d sess., Aug. 1980, Serial 96-15, 159. The estimation of amount of waste produced comes from unpublished 1985 EPA figures, according to Michael Burns, program analyst for the EPA Office of Solid Waste. Burns also said, in a telephone interview on 11 December 1986, that a dearth of data prevents

the EPA from updating the 1980 estimate of the amount of hazardous waste improperly disposed of. He said that many people in the EPA are now concluding that land disposal itself has risks to health and the environment so that even "proper" disposal may not be safe.

60. Congress, Senate Committee on Environment and Public Works, *Health Effects of Toxic Pollution,* 19. Of these dumps, the EPA had, by June 1986, designated 703 as particularly hazardous, putting them on the Superfund's National Priorities List.

61. Ibid., 20.

62. Congress, House Committee on Interstate and Foreign Commerce, Subcommittee on Oversight and Investigation. *Cancer Causing Chemicals in Food,* 95th Cong., 2d sess., 14, 16, 24 Feb., 1978, Serial 95-118, 2.

63. P. Hutt, "Unresolved Issues in the Conflict between Individual Freedom and Government Control of Food Safety," *Ecotoxicology and Environmental Safety* 2(1978): 456.

64. Congress, Senate Committee on Environment and Public Works, *Health Effects of Toxic Pollution,* 8.

65. Samuel S. Epstein, *The Politics of Cancer* (San Francisco: Sierra Club Books, 1978), 65.

66. Gio Batta Gori, "The Regulation of Carcinogenic Hazards," *Science* 208(1980): 259.

67. Richard R. Bates, "Preventing Occupational Cancer," *Environmental Health Perspectives* 28(1979): 306.

68. An alternative interpretation is that permissible exposure levels are not intended to be safe levels. For the statement of principles containing the OSHA and EPA position on thresholds, see Interagency Regulatory Liaison Group (IRLG), Work Group on Risk Assessment, "Scientific Bases for Identification of Potential Carcinogens and Estimation of Risks," *Journal of the National Cancer Institute* 63(1979). The IRLG statement is, "Much has been written about threshold doses for carcinogenic effect, but unfortunately, there is no recognized method for determining their existence. . . . Since threshold doses for carcinogenesis have not been established, a prudent approach from a safety standpoint is to assume that any dose may induce or promote carcinogenesis." The IRLG was disbanded after Reagan became president, and a new interagency group was convened, this one under the Office of Science and Technology Policy. Their statement of principles differs markedly. It says, "At the present stage of knowledge, mechanistic considerations such as DNA repair and other biological responses in general do not prove the existence of, the lack of existence of, or the loca-

tion of a threshold for carcinogenesis." No conclusions are drawn from this statement. See *Federal Register*, 14 Mar. 1985, pt. 2, 10376.

69. Quoted in David Dickson, "OSHA Defends Leap in Carcinogenic Regulations" *Nature* 273(1978): 261.

70. Gori, "Regulation of Carcinogenic Hazards," 259.

71. Bates, "Preventing Occupational Cancer," 307.

72. *Science* 205(1979): 1363–1366. I have quoted his statements here somewhat out of the order in which he made them.

Chapter Three: A Multicausal Solution?

1. Brian MacMahon and Thomas F. Pugh, *Epidemiology: Principles and Methods* (Boston: Little, Brown, 1970), 25.

2. Mervyn Susser, *Causal Thinking in the Health Sciences: Concepts and Strategies of Epidemiology* (New York: Oxford University Press, 1973), 30.

3. See Jackob Najman, "Theories of Disease Causation and the Concept of a General Susceptibility: A Review," *Social Science and Medicine* 14A(1980): 231–237; Nevin S. Scrimshaw, Carl E. Taylor, and John E. Gordon, *Interactions of Nutrition and Infection* (Geneva: World Health Organization, 1968); John Cassel, "The Contribution of the Social Environment to Host Resistance," *American Journal of Epidemiology* 104 (1976): 107–123.

4. See I. Harding-Barlow, "What Is the Status of Arsenic as a Human Carcinogen?" in *Arsenic: Industrial, Biomedical, Environmental Perspectives*, ed. William H. Lederer and Robert J. Fensterheim (New York: Van Nostrand Reinhold, 1983), 203–209.

5. Robert N. Bellah, Richard Madsen, William M. Sullivan, Anne Swidler, and Steven M. Tipton, *Habits of the Heart: Individualism and Commitment in American Life* (Berkeley and Los Angeles: University of California Press, 1985), 277–278.

6. Ibid., 300.

7. John Stuart Mill, *A System of Logic* (Toronto: University of Toronto Press, 1974), 328.

8. For critiques of the germ theory, see René Dubos, *Mirage of Health: Utopias, Progress and Biological Change* (New York: Harper, Colophon, 1959), chap. 4, esp. 101–109; John Powles, "On the Limitation of Modern Medicine," *Science, Medicine, and Man*, 1(1973): 1–50; G. T. Stewart, "Limitations of the Germ Theory," *Lancet*, 18 May 1968; 1077–1081.

9. For an interesting discussion of this point, see John P. Fox, Carrie E. Hall, and Lila R. Elveback, *Epidemiology: Man and Disease* (London: Macmillan, 1970), 31–34.

10. Milton Terris, "The Epidemiologic Tradition," *Public Health Reports* 94(1979): 204.

11. MacMahon and Pugh, *Epidemiology*, 50.

12. Ibid., 25.

13. Few advocates of this new model actually draw weblike diagrams, possibly because the drawings do not help much to visualize the idea, and possibly, too, because they look either too elaborate or too simple. For an example of the latter, see Michael A. Huberman and Matthew B. Miles, "Assessing Local Causality in Qualitative Research," in *Exploring Clinical Methods for Social Research*, ed. David N. Berg and Kenwyn K. Smith (Beverly Hills, Calif.: Sage, 1985), 374. Also, see David F. Fisher, *An Introduction to Epidemiology* (New York: Appleton-Century-Crofts, 1975), frame 35.

14. Talcott Parsons, *The Structure of Social Action* (New York: McGraw-Hill, 1937).

15. Ralf Dahrendorf, "Out of Utopia: Toward a Reorientation of Sociological Analysis," *American Journal of Sociology* 64(1958): 115–127; Alvin W. Gouldner, *The Coming Crisis of Western Sociology* (New York: Basic Books, 1970).

16. Gouldner, *Coming Crisis*, 229, makes a similar criticism: "Parsons' system model . . . begs the question of whether all the variables in a system are equally influential in determining the state of the system as a whole or the condition of any of its parts."

17. Deane Neubauer and Richard Pratt, "The Second Public Health Revolution: A Critical Appraisal," *Journal of Health Politics, Policy and Law* 6(1981): 205–228.

18. This tendency diminished during the years that Eula Bingham ran OSHA under President Carter, although not necessarily in states that had their own OSHA. See Sylvia Tesh, "The Politics of Public Health: Ideology and Disease Causality (Ph.D. diss., University of Hawaii, 1980), chap. 4.

19. John Bryant, *Health and the Developing World* (Ithaca, N.Y.: Cornell University Press, 1969).

20. Nevin Scrimshaw, Carl E. Taylor, and John E. Gordon, *Interactions of Nutrition and Infection* (Geneva: World Health Organization, 1968).

21. Susan George, *How the Other Half Dies: The Real Reasons for World Hunger* (Montclair, N.J.: Allanheld, Osmun, 1977).

22. Fox, Hall, and Elveback, *Epidemiology*, and Stewart, "Limitations of the Germ Theory."

23. The history of malaria control in the Third World is a good example; an excellent book on the subject is Gordon Harrison, *Mosquitoes, Malaria and Man: A History of the Hostilities since 1880* (New York: Dutton, 1978).

24. MacMahon and Pugh, *Epidemiology*, 23.

25. For a discussion of this point, see Fox, Hall, and Elveback, *Epidemiology*, 32.

26. Terris, "Epidemiologic Tradition."

27. Hans Magnus Enzensberger, "A Critique of Political Ecology," *New Left Review* 84(Mar. 1974): 17.

28. Najman, "Theories of Disease," 235.

29. Max Weber, "'Objectivity' in Social Science," in *Readings in the Philosophy of the Social Sciences*, comp. May Brodbeck (New York: Macmillan, 1968), 90.

30. Vaccination directly from smallpox patients has been known since 1729. Edward Jenner developed the practice of vaccinating from cowpox in 1798.

31. Samuel S. Epstein, *The Politics of Cancer* (San Francisco: Sierra Club Books, 1978).

32. Molly Joel Coye, "Crisis: Control in the Workplace," *International Journal of Health Services* 9(1979): 173. Emphasis in the original.

33. Rex Taylor and Annelie Rieger, "Medicine as Social Science: Rudolf Virchow on the Typhus Epidemic in Upper Silesia," *International Journal of Health Services* 15(1985): 547−559.

34. One of Virchow's biographers notes that people frequently mispronounce Virchow's name. "At the banquet in honor of Virchow's eightieth birthday," he says, "Lister greeted him as 'Wirtchow,' while Bacceli addressed him as 'Wirtscho.' When Professor Harnack addressed him as 'Professor Fircho,' the 'f' being pronounced soft as in 'fair,' the 'ch' like 'k' but with the German gutteral, Virchow smiled very pleasantly and turning to a colleague who was nearest to him at the table, said it was the first time he ever remembered hearing his name properly pronounced at a public function." Ralph H. Major, *Classic Descriptions of Disease*, 3d ed. (Springfield, Ill.: Thomas, 1959), 510.

35. Rudolf Virchow, "Mittheilungen über die in Oberschleissen herrschande Typhus-Epidemic," *Archiv für pathologische Anatomie und Physiologie und für klinische Medizin* (Berlin: Hirschwald, 1849), 2:143−322.

36. Quoted in Taylor and Reiger, "Medicine as Social Science," 551.

This article contains what the authors believe to be the only English translation of the final section of Virchow's report.

37. Ibid., 552–554.

38. Ibid., 554.

39. Howard Waitzkin, "The Social Origins of Illness: A Neglected History," *International Journal of Health Services* 11(1981): 77–103.

40. Frederick Engels, "The Condition of the Working Class in England," in *Karl Marx, Frederick Engels: Collected Works* (New York: International Publishers, 1975), 4:298–598.

41. Ibid., 395.

42. Edwin Chadwick, *The Report on the Sanitary Condition of the Labouring Population of Great Britain* (1842; reprint, Edinburgh: Edinburgh University Press, 1965).

43. Engels, "Condition," 457.

44. Ibid., 465–466.

45. Ibid., 466.

46. Ibid., 395.

47. In a less well-known explanation for the wretched conditions among the working class, Engels blamed the Irish immigrants. He labeled the Irish "uncivilized" and "savage." He discerned an "Irish national character" that was oblivious to squalor, and he believed that lack of cleanliness was "the Irishman's second nature." He reasoned thus: "With such a competitor the English working-man has to struggle, with a competitor upon the very lowest plane possible in a civilised country, who for this very reason requires less wages than any other. Nothing else is therefore possible than that . . . the wages of English working-man should be forced down further." Ibid., 392.

48. Ibid., 380, 381.

49. Meredeth Turshen, *The Politics of Public Health* (New Brunswick, N.J.: Rutgers University Press, forthcoming).

50. Evan Stark, "Doctors in Spite of Themselves: The Limits of Radical Health Criticism," *International Journal of Health Services* 12 (1982): 454.

51. Joseph Eyer and Peter Sterling, "Stress-Related Mortality and Social Organization," *Review of Radical Political Economics* 9(Spring 1977): 1–44.

52. Ibid., 17.

53. Peter L. Schnall and Rochelle Kern, "Hypertension in American Society: An Introduction to Historical Materialist Epidemiology," in *The Sociology of Health and Illness: Critical Perspectives*, ed. Peter Conrad and Rochelle Kern (New York: St. Martin's, 1981).

54. Ibid., 114. Emphasis in the original.

55. Robert Karasek, "Job Decision Latitude, Job Demands, and Cardiovascular Disease: A Prospective Study of Swedish Men," *American Journal of Public Health* 71(1981): 649–705.

56. Ibid., 702.

57. Vicente Navarro, "Work, Ideology, and Science: The Case of Medicine," in *Health and Work under Capitalism: An International Perspective*, ed. Vicente Navarro and Daniel M. Berman (Farmingdale, N.Y.: Baywood, 1983), 14.

58. For examples of analyses that implicitly discuss disease in terms of personal failure, see Margaret M. Heckler, "Healthy Mothers, Healthy Babies: A Goal We Can All Attain," *Public Health Reports* 98 (1983): 529; David D. Rutstein, "Controlling the Communicable and the Man Made Diseases," *New England Journal of Medicine* 304(1981): 1422–1424; S. Heydon and J. G. Fodor, "Industrial Cancer Education and Screening for 19,000 Cannon Mills Employees," *Journal of Chronic Diseases* 34(1981): 225–231.

Chapter Four: Cuba and Health Promotion

1. E. Richard Brown and Glen Elgin Margo, "Health Education: Can the Reformers Be Reformed?" *International Journal of Health Services* 8(1978): 3–26.

2. In 1984 the Cuban Institute of Tropical Medicine (Pedro Kouri), a branch of the Ministry of Public Health, invited my husband as a consultant on dengue fever. The invitation was later extended to include me, and the institute very kindly arranged for me a full schedule of interviews and trips.

3. Jorge Valdes-Brito Aldereguia and Jorge Henriquez Aldereguia, "Health Statistics of the Cuban Population," *International Journal of Health Services* 13(1983): 479–486. The first author is director general of the Institute for Health Development, Havana.

4. Vicente Navarro, "Health, Health Services, and Health Planning in Cuba," *International Journal of Health Services* 2(1972): 397–432; Milton I. Roemer, "Health Development and Political Policy: The Lesson of Cuba," *Journal of Health Politics, Policy and Law* 4(1980): 570–580; Dudley Seers, *Cuba: The Economic and Social Revolution* (Chapel Hill: University of North Carolina Press, 1964).

5. According to 1983 figures from the Cuban Ministry of Public Health, the main causes of death per 100,000 people were heart dis-

ease, 171.7; malignant tumors, 113.0; and cerebrovascular diseases, 56.5. Few people realize, however, that despite the high rate of infectious disease before 1959, Cuba's health profile was excellent compared with other Latin American nations. In fact, by the 1950s, cardiovascular diseases and cancer were already the major causes of mortality. See Susan Shroeder, *Cuba: A Handbook of Historical Statistics* (Boston: Hall, 1982); and *Cuba 1968: Supplement to the Statistical Abstract of Latin America* (University of California at Los Angeles, Latin American Center, 1970).

6. Sarah Conover, Stephen Donovan, and Ezra Susser, "Reflections on Health Care in Cuba, *Lancet*, 1 Nov. 1980, 958–960.

7. For descriptions of the mechanical model, see Samuel Osherson and Lorna Amara Singham, "The Machine Metaphor in Medicine," in *Social Contexts of Health, Illness, and Patient Care*, ed. Eliot Mishler (Cambridge: Cambridge University Press, 1981); and John Powels, "On the Limitations of Modern Medicine," *Science, Medicine and Man* 1(1973): 1–30.

8. This was one of five formal interviews arranged for me by MINSAP. Interviews lasted about two hours and I taped most of them. Besides this one with about six people at a Havana policlinic, I had interviews with other groups of staff members at policlinics in the city of Matanzas and the small nearby town of Union de Reyes, with the national director of health education, and with the director of health education for the city of Havana. These interviews were all in Spanish. The reader should know, however, that my Spanish was rusty and that this fact influenced the interaction between me and the people I talked with. The interviews were, of course, augmented by many informal conversations with my Cuban hosts.

9. Most of the campaigns involve either sanitation of one sort or another—from tips for food handlers to warnings against dumping garbage in vacant lots—or exhortations to visit the doctor for a pap smear, for immunizations, for possible blood poisoning, and so on.

10. Raul Mazorra Zamora, *Para tu Salud: Corre o Camina* (Havana: Ministerio de Cultura, Científico, 1983), 25. This and all other translations are mine.

11. For a description of the general sports program, see John Griffiths, "Sport: The People's Right," in *Cuba: The Second Decade*, ed. John Griffiths and Peter Griffiths (London: Writers & Readers, 1979), 247–260.

12. Mazorra Zamora, *Para tu Salud*, 31.

13. Fidel Castro, *Discursos en Tres Congresos* (Havana: Editora Politica, 1982), 3.

14. Mazorra Zamora, *Para tu Salud*, 5.

15. Movimiento de Caminantes de Cuba, *Caminar es Salud* (Havana: Habana Dirección Nacional de Recreación, n.d.).

16. Educación Para la Salud, *La Preparación Física: Fuente de Salud* (Havana: MINSAP, n.d.).

17. Karl Marx, *Preface to a Contribution to the Critique of Political Economy* (New York: International Publishers, 1970), 20.

18. Jakub Netoplik, "El Modo de Vida Socialista y el Desarrolo del Hombre," in *El Modo de Vida Socialista* (Havana: Ciencias Sociales, 1983). Reprinted from *Sotsialisticheskii obra zhizn* (Moscow: Progress, 1979). I chose this particular quotation from many possible interpretations because I bought the book in which it appears in a Havana bookstore, so it carries the imprimatur of the Cuban government.

19. Mazorra Zamora, *Para tu Salud*, 6.

20. *Morbidity and Mortality Weekly Report*, 8 June 1984.

21. A. Chesterfield-Evans, "BUGA-UP (Billboard Utilization Graffitists Against Unhealthy Promotions): An Australian Movement to End Cigarette Advertising," *New York State Journal of Medicine* 83(1983): 1333–1334.

22. R. C. Bates, "Doctors Who Smoke," *New York State Journal of Medicine* 83(1983): 1294; A. Blum, "Using Athletes to Push Tobacco to Children," ibid., 1365–1367.

23. M. Murray, A. V. Swan, and G. Clarke, "Long Term Effect of a School Based Antismoking Program," *Journal of Epidemiology and Community Health* 38 (1981): 247–252.

24. M. Coleman, "The Research Smokescreen: Moving from Academic Debates to Action on Smoking," *New York State Journal of Medicine* 83(1983): 1280–1281; G. C. Godber, "A Global View: Health versus Greed," ibid., 1248–1249.

25. J. E. Rose, S. Ananda, and M. E. Jarvik, "Cigarette Smoking during Anxiety-Provoking and Monotonous Tasks," *Addictive Behaviors* 8 (1983): 353–359.

26. W. Bennett, "The Nicotine Fix," *Rhode Island Medical Journal* 66(1983): 455–458.

27. There are other interpretations. According to one observer, sometime in the 1970s Castro was "the first to quit smoking when the people were asked to cut down on their own consumption in order to increase tobacco exports." See Marta Harnecker, *Cuba: Dictatorship or Democracy?* (Westport, Conn.: Hill, 1980), 89. In 1986, however, the publication of New York's Center for Cuban Studies noted, "During the opening of a children's hospital on August 26, [Castro] mentioned

that he had not touched tobacco since August 1985." *Cuba Update* 7 (Fall 1986): 23.

28. Tobacco no longer has a central place in the economy. Before the revolution the Cuban economy was based on three products: sugar, tobacco, and rum. Today sugar is still king, but the production of nickel, citrus fruits, and fish outstrip tobacco and rum in importance. In 1980 exports from the sugar industry brought in over three billion pesos; mineral exports amounted to nearly two hundred million; fishing was over ninety million pesos; and the tobacco industry brought in about sixty-five million pesos. See Comite Estatal de Estadisticas, *Anuario Estadístico de Cuba 1980* (Havana, 1982), and Susan Shroeder, *Cuba: A Handbook of Historical Statistics* (Boston: Hall, 1982).

29. Managers are also liable for fines if, on reinspection, MINSAP industrial hygienists find the workplace still hazardous. These fines, also, are paid by the managers personally. (A peso is worth about a dollar.)

30. Robin Alexander and Pamela K. Anderson, "Pesticide Use, Alternatives and Workers' Health in Cuba," *International Journal of Health Services* 14(1984): 31–41; Manuel R. Gomez, "Occupational Health in Cuba," *American Journal of Public Health* 71(1981): 520–524; Antonio Granda and Jesus Cabrera Perez, "Estado Actual de la Salud Ocupacional en Cuba" (MINSAP, Instituto de Medicina del Trabajo, Havana, March 1984).

31. Schroeder, *Cuba.*

32. William Haddon, Jr., "Advances in the Epidemiology of Injuries as a Basis for Public Policy," *Public Health Reports* 95(1980): 418–421; Leon Robertson, *Injuries: Causes, Control Strategies, and Public Policy* (Lexington, Mass.: Heath, 1983); Susan P. Baker, Brian O'Neill, and Ronald S. Karpf, *Injury Fact Book* (Lexington, Mass.: Heath, 1984).

33. Dirección de Educación para la Salud, *Temas Populares de Salud* (Havana: MINSAP, 1975), 81–83.

34. R. S. Paffenbarger, Jr., and R. T. Hyde, "Exercise as Protection against Heart Attacks," *New England Journal of Medicine* 302(1980): 1026–1027; Kenneth H. Cooper, Michael L. Pollock, Randolph P. Martin, Steve R. White, Ardell C. Linnerud, and Andrew Jackson, "Physical Fitness Levels vs. Selected Coronary Risk Factors," *Journal of the American Medical Association* 236(1976): 166–169; G. H. Hartung, "Physical Activity and Coronary Heart Disease: A Review," *American Corrective Therapy Journal* 31(1977): 110–115.

35. Theodore D. Sterling, "Filtering Information about Occupa-

tion, Smoking, and Disease," *Journal of Chronic Diseases* 37(1984): 227–230.

36. Alexander and Anderson, "Pesticide Use."

37. Bicycles are scarce in Cuba.

38. Shlomo Avineri, *Social and Political Thought of Karl Marx* (Cambridge: Cambridge University Press, 1968), 92.

39. Harnecker, *Cuba: Dictatorship or Democracy*; Griffiths and Griffiths, *Cuba: The Second Decade.*

Chapter Five: Air Traffic Control and Stress

1. John Hughes, *The Philosophy of Social Research* (New York: Longman, 1980); Anthony Giddens, *Studies in Social and Political Theory* (New York: Basic Books, 1977); Barry Barnes, *Interests and the Growth of Knowledge* (London: Routledge & Kegan Paul, 1977).

2. Robert D. Caplan, Sidney Cobb, John R. French, Jr., R. Van Harrison, and S. R. Pinneau, Jr., *Job Demands and Worker Health: Main Effects and Occupational Differences*, HEW Publication No. (NIOSH) 75-160 (Washington, D.C.: National Institute of Occupational Safety and Health, 1975); E. M. Leeper, "It's Clear That Stress Can Lead to Illness, but It's Not Clear How," *News Report*, National Academy of Sciences, July 1982; G. R. Eisdorfer and C. Eisdorfer, eds., *Stress and Human Health: Analysis and Implications of Research*, Springer Series on Psychiatry 1, for the National Academy of Sciences, Institute of Medicine, Committee to Study Research on Stress in Health and Disease (New York: Springer, 1982). J. Rabkin and E. L. Struening, "Life Events, Stress and Illness," *Science* 194(1976): 1013.

3. *The Nation* 233(1981): 696–698; ibid.; *In These Times* 5, no. 32 (1981); ibid., no. 33 (1981); ibid., no. 34 (1981); ibid., no. 36 (1981); ibid. 6, no. 4 (1981).

4. Daniel Berman, *Death on the Job: Occupational Health and Safety Struggle in the United States* (New York: Monthly Review Press, 1978); Samuel S. Epstein, *The Politics of Cancer* (San Francisco: Sierra Club Books, 1978); Paul Brodeur, *Expendable Americans* (New York: Viking, 1974).

5. Garfield, "Alienated Labor, Stress and Coronary Disease," *International Journal of Health Services* 10(1980): 551–561; Marianne Frankenhaeuser, "Coping with Stresses at Work," *International Journal of Health Services* 11(1981): 491–510.

6. Stanley Aronowitz thinks this is consistent with American labor's mistaken separation of economic struggle from political struggle. See his *Working Class Hero* (New York: Pilgrim, 1983).

7. Congress, House Committee on Post Office and Civil Service, Subcommittee on Civil Service, *Air Traffic Controllers and Flight Service Station Specialists*, 96th Cong., 1st sess., 26, 30 June, 2, 13 July, 1979, Serial 96-37, 1.

8. Ibid., 17.

9. Ibid., 68–69.

10. Ibid., 69.

11. Ibid., 69.

12. Hans Selye, *Stress in Health and Disease* (Reading, Mass.: Butterworth, 1976), 14.

13. Hans Selye, *The Stress of Life* (Toronto: McGraw-Hill, 1956).

14. Selye, *Stress in Health*, 14–15.

15. Ibid., 14–15.

16. R. H. Rosenmann, M. Friedman, and R. A. Strauss, "A Predictive Study of CHD," *Journal of the American Medical Association* 189 (1964): 15; C. D. Jenkins, "Psychologic and Social Precursors of Coronary Disease," *New England Journal of Medicine* 284(1971): 244, 307.

17. C. L. Cooper, *The Stress Check: Coping with the Stresses of Life and Work* (Englewood Cliffs, N.J.: Prentice-Hall, 1981).

18. E. G. Jaco, "Mental Illness in Response to Stress," in *Social Stress*, ed. S. Levine and N. A. Scotch (Chicago: Aldine, 1973), 211.

19. Caplan, *Job Demands*, 3.

20. B. Dohrenwend and B. D. Dohrenwend, eds., *Stressful Life Events: Their Nature and Effects* (New York: Wiley, 1974); T. H. Holmes and R. H. Rahe, "The Social Readjustment Rating Scale," *Journal of Psychosomatic Research* 11(1967): 213.

21. Aaron Back, *Occupational Stress: The Inside Story* (Oakland, Calif.: Institute for Labor and Mental Health, 1981); Robert Karasek, Dean Baker, Frank Marxer, Anders Ahlbom, and Tores Theorell, "Job Decision, Latitude, Job Demands, and Cardiovascular Disease: A Prospective Study of Swedish Men," *American Journal of Public Health* 71(1981): 694.

22. Aronowitz, *Working Class Hero*, 67.

23. Joseph Eyer and Peter Sterling, "Stress-Related Mortality and Social Organization," *Review of Radical Political Economics* 9(Spring 1977): 31.

24. S. Gordon, "Workplace Fantasies," *Working Papers for a New Society* 111(Sept./Oct. 1980): 36–41.

25. Of course it is true that the words *book* and *cloud* likewise stand for whatever we want them to. But for ordinary use, we agree on prototypical meanings for these words. We only disagree about differences at the margins. When does a book deviate enough from the norm to become a pamphlet? When does a cloud become haze? "Stress," being an abstraction, cannot have a prototype in this way.

26. See Eyer and Sterling, "Stress-Related Mortality," for example.

27. Congress, House Committee on Post Office and Civil Service, Subcommittee on Compensation and Employees Benefits, *Oversight on Grievances of Air Traffic Control Specialists*, 97th Cong., 1st sess., 30 Apr., 1981, 15.

28. Ibid.

29. Ibid., 16.

30. Ibid., 17.

31. Ibid., 18.

32. R. M. Rose, C. D. Jenkins, and M. W. Hurst, *Air Traffic Controllers Health Change Study: A Prospective Investigation of Physical, Psychological and Work-related Changes* (Boston: Boston University School of Medicine, 1978).

33. Congress, House Committee on Post Office and Civil Service, *Oversight on Grievances*, 42–43.

34. Ibid., 44.

35. Rose, Jenkins, and Hurst, *Air Traffic Controllers*, 17.

36. Ibid., 623. The bulk of this book is devoted to reports on the battery of physical examinations and psychological questionnaires administered to the controllers. These included the California Psychological Inventory, the Jenkins Activity Survey, and the Sixteen Personality Factors Questionnaire; a job attitude questionnaire created specifically for this study; a Review of Life Experience scale developed from the Holmes and Rahe Schedule of Life Experiences and the Paykel, Uhlenhuth, and Prusoff questionnaire; the Profile of Mood States; the Zung Anxiety and Depression Scales; a health history questionnaire and a monthly health review questionnaire; physical and psychological examinations approximately every nine months at Boston University; and on-the-job measurements of blood pressure and collection of blood samples for hormone assays.

37. Ibid., 634.

38. Ibid., 627. Emphasis added.

39. Ibid., 626. Emphasis added.

40. Ibid., 636.

41. Ibid., 616.

42. Ibid., 636.

43. Ibid., 17.

44. Ibid., 21.

45. Allan Young, "The Discourse on Stress and the Reproduction of Conventional Knowledge," *Social Science and Medicine* 14B(1980): 133–146.

46. Rose, Jenkins, and Hurst, *Air Traffic Controllers*, 14.

47. Ibid., 634.

48. Ibid., 636.

49. Congress, House Committee on Public Works and Transportation, *Aviation Safety (PATCO Walkout)*, 97th Cong., 2d sess., 18, 19, 25 June, 16 Dec., 1981 and 25 Mar., 1982, Serial 97-78.

50. Ibid., 605.

51. Ibid., 606.

52. Ibid., 639.

53. Ibid., 644.

54. "We feel that some union activities may inadvertently have contributed to the alienation and divisiveness many controllers experience in their ongoing adversarial relations with the agency." Rose, Jenkins, and Hurst, *Air Traffic Controllers*, 16.

55. Congress, House Committee on Post Office and Civil Service, *Oversight on Grievances*, 667.

56. Ibid., 668.

57. Ibid., 682.

58. Ibid., 683.

59. Karasek et al., "Job Decision."

60. Actually, the controllers did commission one study. They asked the Western Institute for Occupational/Environmental Sciences, the director of which was the PATCO "health advisor," to critique the Rose report. The resulting fifty-three-page unpublished paper challenges some of the Rose methodology and interpretation but was apparently of little use to the controllers. None of them mentioned it during congressional hearings. See D. Roth et al., "A Critique of the Air Traffic Controller Health Change Study (Berkeley, Calif.: Western Institute for Occupational/Environmental Sciences, n.d.).

61. Rose, Jenkins, and Hurst, *Air Traffic Controllers*, 636.

62. Quoted in L. Hinkle, "The Concept of 'Stress' in the Biological and Social Sciences," *Science, Medicine and Man* 1(1973): 35.

63. Charles E. Lindblom, "Another State of Mind," *American Political Science Review* 76(Mar. 1982): 9–21; A. W. Gouldner, *The Coming Crisis of Western Sociology* (New York: Basic Books, 1980).

Chapter Six: Vietnam Veterans and Agent Orange

1. Constance Holden, "Agent Orange Furor Continues to Build," *Science* 205 (1979):770–772; Marc Leepson, "Agent Orange: The Continuing Debate," *Editorial Research Reports* 11 (July 6, 1984): 491–508.

2. Comptroller General of the United States, *Ground Troops in South Vietnam Were in Areas Sprayed with Herbicide Orange*, Report B159451. Issued by GAO 16 Nov. 1979, at request of Senator Charles Percy.

3. Ibid.

4. Congress, House Committee on Veterans' Affairs, Subcommittee on Medical Facilities, *Oversight Hearing to Receive Testimony on Agent Orange* (hereafter cited as *Hearing on Agent Orange*) 96th Cong., 2d sess., 22 July, 1980, 190.

5. Ibid., 58, 127.

6. Quoted in Jeffrey L. Fox, "Agent Orange Study Is like a Chameleon," *Science* 223(1984): 1156. The Ranch Hand report itself is still ongoing and unpublished. The first portion, written by George D. Lathrop, is called "An Epidemiological Investigation of Health Effects in Air Force Personnel following Exposure to Herbicides: Baseline Morbidity Results." It is dated 24 Feb. 1984.

7. J. David Erickson, Joseph Mulinare, Philip W. McClain, Terry G. Fitch, Levy M. James, Anne B. McClearn, and Myron J. Adams, Jr., "Vietnam Veterans' Risks for Fathering Babies with Birth Defects," *Journal of the American Medical Association* 252(1984): 903–912.

8. Council on Scientific Affairs, American Medical Association, "Health Effects of Agent Orange and Dioxin Contaminants," *Journal of the American Medical Association* 248(1983): 1895–1897.

9. Philip H. Abelson, "Chlorinated Dioxins," editorial in *Science* 220(1983): 4604.

10. Editorial note, *Journal of the American Medical Association* 251 (1984): 1139.

11. Lynne Moody, William E. Halperin, Marilyn A. Fingerhut, and Philip J. Landrigan, "The Chronic Health Effects of Occupational Exposure to Dioxin: Unanswered Questions," editorial in *American Journal of Industrial Medicine* 5(1984): 157–160.

12. P. S. Honchar and W. E. Halperin, "2,4,5-T, Trichlorophenol, and Soft Tissue Sarcoma," letter in *Lancet*, 31 Jan. 1981, 268.

13. Theodore D. Sterling, "Health Effects of Dioxin," letter to *Science* 223(1984): 1201.

14. Quoted in Michael Mulkay, *Science and the Sociology of Knowledge* (London: Allen & Unwin, 1980), 20.

15. T. H. Huxley, in ibid., 15.

16. J. Bronowski, quoted in *Classics in Science*, ed. E. N. Da C. Andrade (Edinburgh: Philosophical Library, 1960), 215.

17. James Bryant Conant, *Science and Common Sense* (New Haven, Conn.: Yale University Press, 1951), 8.

18. *Hearing on Agent Orange*, 1.

19. Ibid., 51.

20. Congress, House Committee on Sciences and Technology, Subcommittee on Natural Resources, Agriculture Research and Environment, *Dioxin: The Impact on Human Health*, 98th Cong., 1st sess., 30 June, 13, 28 July, 1983, No. 78, 3.

21. Ibid., 3.

22. *Hearing on Agent Orange*, 283.

23. Ibid.; Philip Caputo, *Rumor of War* (New York: Ballantine, 1977); Michael Uhl and Tod Ensign, *GI Guinea Pigs: How the Pentagon Exposed Our Troops to Dangers More Deadly Than War* (New York: Playboy, 1980); Michael Herr, *Dispatches* (New York: Knopf, 1977).

24. Uhl and Ensign, *GI Guinea Pigs*; Interviews with staff of Agent Orange Veterans Inc., Stamford, Conn.

25. The most available example is the fifty-minute documentary from Green Mountain Productions called "The Secret Agent." It was widely shown on public television during 1985 and won an award that year at the New York City Film Festival.

26. *Hearing on Agent Orange*, 282.

27. Ibid., 273.

28. Frank McCarthy, head of Agent Orange Victims, Inc., in presentation to Yale University School of Public Health students, 25 Jan. 1985.

29. *New York Times*, 9 August 1984.

30. The story of Paul Reutershan, the founder of Agent Orange

Veterans Inc., provides one example. Not long before he died of stomach cancer in 1978, he wrote a widely publicized letter to President Carter in which he said, "At 28 years of age, in the hospital with terminal cancer, and the many doctors not being able to find the cause, this [Agent Orange] could be the only logical, possible answer." In its story on Reutershan, the *New York Times*, 12 Oct. 1978, wrote, "Because he had never drunk or smoked and because he had always liked simple things, Reutershan became convinced that his health problems stemmed from exposure to agent orange." And according to the Gannett Westchester, New York, newspapers (5 May 1979), "He could not understand how it happened to him . . . could not accept that he had developed cancer without a clear cut cause."

31. Laura Conti, *Visto da Seveso: L'evento straordinario e l'ordinario amministrazione* (Milan: Feltrinelli, 1977); quoted in Gianna Pomata, "Seveso: Safety in Numbers?" *Radical Science Journal* 9(1979): 69–81.

32. Adeline Gordon Levine, *Love Canal: Science, Politics, and People* (Lexington, Mass.: Lexington Books, 1982).

33. William Broad and Nicholas Wade, *Betrayers of the Truth: Fraud and Deceit in the Halls of Science* (New York: Simon & Schuster, 1982).

34. Ian D. Clark, "Expert Advice in the Controversy about Supersonic Transport in the United States," *Minerva* 12(1974): 419.

35. Alvin M. Weinberg, "Science and Trans-Science," *Minerva* 10 (1972): 209–222.

36. Ibid., 218–219.

37. Alfred S. Evans, "Causation and Disease: The Henle-Koch Postulates Revisited," *Yale Journal of Biology and Medicine* 49(1976): 175–195.

38. Brendan Gillespie, Dave Eva, and Ron Johnston, "Carcinogenic Risk Assessment in the United States and Britain: The Case of Aldrin and Dieldrin," *Social Studies of Science* 9(1979): 265–301.

39. Stanley Joel Reisor, "Smoking and Health: The Congress and Causality," in *Knowledge and Power*, ed. Sanford A. Lakoff (New York: Free Press, 1966).

40. For the cancer policy of the Interagency Regulatory Liaison Group (consisting of the Consumer Product Safety Commission, the Environmental Protection Agency, the Food and Drug Administration, and the Occupational Safety and Health Administration) see "Scientific Bases for Identification of Potential Carcinogens and Estimation of Risks," *Journal of the National Cancer Institute* 63(1979). For a later cancer policy, this one by the Office of Science and Technology, see "Chemical

Carcinogens: A Review of the Science and Its Associated Principles," *Federal Register* 50(1985): 10372–10442.

41. Thomas Kuhn, *The Structure of Scientific Revolutions* (Chicago: University of Chicago Press, 1970), 111–112.

42. Ibid., 121.

43. Stephen Toulmin, "The Construal of Reality," in *The Politics of Interpretation*, ed. W. J. T. Mitchell (Chicago: University of Chicago Press, 1983), 102.

44. Ibid., 112.

45. Evelyn Fox Keller, "Feminism and Science," in *Feminist Theory: A Critique of Ideology*, ed. Nannerl O. Keohane, Michelle Z. Rosaldo, and Barbara C. Gilip (Chicago: University of Chicago Press, 1982), 125.

46. Michael Mulkay, *Science and the Sociology of Knowledge* (London: Allen & Unwin, 1979), 114.

47. Ibid., 115. Emphasis added.

48. *New York Times*, 18 Apr. 1986.

49. Honchar and Halperin, "2,4,5-T, Trichlorophenol."

50. Mulkay, *Sociology of Knowledge*, 117–118.

Chapter Seven: Individualism and Science

1. Daniel E. Koshland, Jr., "Spanking, Reason, and the Environment," *Science* 234(1986): 409.

2. Karl Marx and Friedrich Engels, *The German Ideology* (1846; reprint, New York: International Publishers, 1970), chap. 1, pt. 3, art. 3.

3. Kenneth M. Dolbeare and Patricia Dolbeare, *American Ideologies: The Competing Political Beliefs of the 1970s*, 3d ed. (Skokie, Ill.: Rand McNally, 1976), 2–3.

4. Karl Mannheim, "Ideology and the Sociology of Knowledge," in *Readings in the Philosophy of the Social Sciences*, ed. May Brodbeck (New York: Macmillan, 1968), 121–122.

5. Georg Lukács, *History and Class Consciousness* (Cambridge: MIT Press, 1968), 50.

6. For examples, see Michel Foucault, *Madness and Civilization: A History of Insanity in the Age of Reason* (New York: Random House, 1965); or Joseph R. Gusfield, *The Culture of Public Problems: Drinking-Driving and the Symbolic Order* (Chicago: University of Chicago Press, 1981).

7. Steven Lukes, *Individualism* (New York: Harper & Row, 1973).

8. The preamble to the Charter of the United Nations states that the signers "reaffirm faith in fundamental human rights, in the dignity and worth of the human person, [and] in the equal rights of men and women." Article I reiterates the goal of "friendly relations among nations based on respect for the principle of equal rights and self determination of peoples."

9. Lukes, *Individualism*, 73.

10. Ibid., 80.

11. Ibid., 94.

12. Ibid., 88.

13. Ibid., 157.

14. For descriptions of early regulations, see Michael W. Flinn, Introduction in Edwin Chadwick, *The Report of the Sanitary Condition of the Labouring Population of Great Britain* (1842; reprint, Edinburgh: Edinburgh University Press, 1965); also S. G. Checkland, *The Rise of Industrial Society in England 1815—1885* (London: Longmans, Green, 1966); and Arthur J. Taylor, *Laissez Faire and State Intervention in Nineteenth Century Britain* (London: Macmillan, 1972).

15. Nassau Senior, after witnessing the living conditions of London's poor, concluded that "with all our reverence for the principle of non-interference, we cannot doubt that in this matter it has been pushed too far. We believe that both ground landlord and the speculating builder ought to be compelled by law, though it should cost them a percentage of their rent and profit, to take measures which shall prevent the towns which they create from being centres of disease." Quoted by Flinn, Introduction, in Chadwick, *Report*, 39.

16. William Ryan, *Blaming the Victim* (New York: Random House, Vintage, 1972).

17. Ibid., 23—24. Emphasis in the original.

18. Alan Garfinkel, *The Ethics of Explanation* (New Haven, Conn.: Yale University Press, 1981), 152—153.

19. See Mark MacCarthy, "A Review of Some Normative and Conceptual Issues in Occupational Safety and Health," *Boston College Environmental Affairs Law Review* 9(1981): 773—814.

20. Colin Norman and David Dickson, "The Aftermath of Chernobyl," *Science* 233(1986): 1141—1143.

21. Alasdair MacIntyre, "Durkheim's Call to Order," *New York Review of Books* 7 Mar. 1974, 26; quoted in Peter Steinfels, "Individualism: No Exit," *Hastings Center Studies* 2(Sept., 1974): 10.

22. Lukes, *Individualism*, 101.

23. R. C. Lewontin, Steven Rose, and Leon J. Kamin, *Not in Our Genes: Biology, Ideology, and Human Nature* (New York: Pantheon, 1984), 46.

24. Lawrence K. Altman, "Can Vaccine Prevent Cancer?" *New York Times*, 6 Dec. 1983, C3.

25. Thomas Colton, *Statistics in Medicine* (Boston: Little, Brown, 1974), 117.

26. Elizabeth Fee, "Is Feminism a Threat to Scientific Objectivity?" *International Journal of Women's Studies* 4(1981): 384–385.

27. Barrington Moore, Jr., "Tolerance and the Scientific Outlook," in *A Critique of Pure Tolerance*, Robert Paul Wolff, Barrington Moore, Jr., and Herbert Marcuse (Boston: Beacon, 1965), 64.

28. Carole Vance, "The Female Body and the Social Construction of Sexuality" (Paper presented at the Women's Studies Lecture Series, Yale University, 14 Oct. 1985).

29. Leslie Rado, "The Body: The Intellectual Project and the Real Thing" (Paper presented at the Whitney Humanities Center, Yale University, 10 Dec. 1986).

30. Stephen Toulmin, "Can Science and Ethics Be Reconnected? *Hastings Center Report* 9, no. 3(1979): 28.

31. R. C. Lewontin, "The Corpse in the Elevator," *New York Review of Books*, 20 Jan. 1983.

32. Lewontin, Rose, and Kamins, *Not in Our Genes*, 75.

33. Sandra Harding, *The Science Question in Feminism* (Ithaca, N.Y.: Cornell University Press, 1986).

34. Harding, *Science Question*, 249.

35. Ibid., 250.

Index

accidents, 34; traffic (in Cuba), 96–97. *See also* occupational safety and health
Ackerknecht, Erwin, 15
adolescent pregnancies, in Cuba, 87
Agent Orange, 131; birth defects and, 134, 138–139; cancer and, 131, 134, 144–146; exposure to (in Vietnam), 133; facts and meaning regarding, 132–141; political context of debate on, 151–152; scientific answer about disease causation by, 148–149; scientific disagreement and, 133–137, 141–149; toxic effects from, 134–135, 138; values and research on, 149; veterans' response to studies of, 139–141. *See also* dioxin
Ahrens, E. H., Jr., 44
AIDS, 40, 80–81
air and atmosphere: disease and, 25–29, 45; pollution of, 51, 56–57. *See also* miasma theory of disease causality
air traffic controllers: job of, 120–122; stress and, 110,

111–113, 115–126, 128, 129; strike by, 108–111
alcoholism: in Soviet Union, 77
American Industrial Hygiene Council, 54
American Medical Association: and Agent Orange, 134
apartheid, 77
asbestos, 49, 69
authoritarianism, 20; disease causality beliefs and, 16–17
avoidance as preventive measure, 12–13

Bates, Richard, 54, 55
Beecher, Lyman, 20, 21
behavior change, voluntary (in Cuba), 92
Bentham, Jeremy, 30
Berliner, Howard, 47
black plague. *See* bubonic plague
Borroto, Jorge, 87, 93, 94
bubonic plague, 10, 11, 13

cancer: in Cuba, 193n5, diet and, 41, 42–44, 55; dioxin and Agent Orange and, 131, 134, 144–146; mortality from, 33; as multi-caused, 59; policy,

207

CPSIA information can be obtained at www.ICGtesting.com
Printed in the USA
LVOW10s1801010216

473190LV00001B/141/P